order to intervene in the course of history." Along with today's renewed interest in the spiritual core of Christianity has come an increased concern with the shaping of religious doctrines by history, and the interconnections between Christianity and western civilization. Those areas of American religious thought now fruitlessly concerned with the "death of God," the author holds, would benefit from exposure to the viewpoint represented by Troeltsch and Harnack. In its clear presentation of these two major figures, Professor Pauck's book is an attack upon the stronghold of ignorance about the Christian heritage that has, he contends, impoverished and isolated the churches in this country.

Wilhelm Pauck, presently Distinguished Professor of Church History at Vanderbilt University, has taught history and theology at Chicago Theological Seminary, the University of Chicago, Union Theological Seminary, New York, and Columbia University. He is the author of many books, including *Luther's Lectures on Romans* and *The Heritage of the Reformation*.

Harnack and Troeltsch

HARNACK

AND

TROELTSCH

Two Historical Theologians

WILHELM PAUCK

NEW YORK

OXFORD UNIVERSITY PRESS

1968

Printed in the United States of America

To Marion

Preface

The following biographical sketches constituted the content of the Tipple Lectures which I delivered at Drew Theological Seminary on 28–31 March 1967. An earlier version of the essay on Harnack served as the Presidential Address presented to the American Theological Society in 1964. It was published in the volume entitled *Handbook of Protestant Theologians,* in 1965. I wish to thank the editors of Meridian Books and the World Publishing Company for permitting me to use the substance of this essay in this volume in a somewhat changed and enlarged form.

During a conversation with Mr. Wilbur D. Ruggles, vice-president and editor of Religious Books of the Oxford University Press, New York, it occurred to me to add to my characterization of Harnack and Troeltsch, two pieces of writing which each of these distinguished scholars devoted to the other. One is the oration which Adolf von Harnack delivered at the funeral service for his friend Ernst Troeltsch in 1923, and the other is the article which Troeltsch contributed to the *Festgabe* which his colleagues dedicated to Harnack on his seventieth birthday in 1921. Each of these contains a telling appreciation of one scholar for the other. I have therefore translated them from the German. I am sure that the readers of this little volume will regard them as an enrichment of what I have to say about these gentlemen.

Wilhelm Pauck

Vanderbilt University
Nashville, Tennessee
September 1967

Contents

Harnack and Troeltsch

Adolf von Harnack

I

Adolf von Harnack was born on 7 May 1851 in the Baltic city of Dorpat in Livonia, which was then and is now again a Russian province. His forebears had come there from Germany. His paternal grandfather, a tailor, hailed from East Prussia; his maternal grandfather, a professor in the University of Dorpat and, for many years, its rector, was a native Westphalian. His father, Theodosius Harnack, a strict Lutheran with pietistic leanings, was a professor of practical and systematic theology, first in Dorpat, then for thirteen years (1853–1866) in Erlangen, Germany, and then, again, for the rest of his life in Dorpat (he died in 1889).

Harnack and his three brothers (they were all unusually gifted) were educated in Erlangen and Dorpat. In October 1872 Adolf left home in order to complete his studies in the University of Leipzig.[1]

1. Hans Lietzmann writes in a commemorative article in *Theologische Literaturzeitung* 76 (1951): "When as a young student I became acquainted with Harnack in Venice, he told me one evening during an unforgettable conversation about his upbringing. As if he were telling a fairy-tale he said: 'We were four brothers, and when we left home, our father gave each of us one thousand dollars and told us that we should make good. All four of us did make good—and I still have the thousand dollars.'" On Harnack's

3

In 1873 he wrote and published his doctoral dissertation on an early Gnostic text. Shortly thereafter (1874),
he began his academic career as a church historian, first
as a *Privatdozent* (1874), and then as a professor-
extraordinary (1876) in Leipzig. In 1879 he was appointed to a professorship in Giessen. From there he
moved to Marburg (1886). Two years later he was
called to the University of Berlin. By then he had already acquired fame as a teacher, researcher, author,
critic, and as an organizer of scientific projects.[2] This
call was opposed by the Supreme Council of the Evangelical Church. As the highest office of the Prussian
state church, it was entitled to exercise a veto right of
sorts on appointments to the theological chairs in the
universities. However, both the faculty and the Minister
of Education strongly desired Harnack's appointment.
On their recommendation and on that of Chancellor
Bismarck and his cabinet, Emperor William II, then at
the very beginning of his reign, overruled the church

relation with his father, see C. Wayne Glick, *The Reality of Christianity: A Study of A. von Harnack as Historian and Theologian*
(New York, 1967), pp. 23–28. Glick also stresses Harnack's dependence upon his main academic teacher in Dorpat, Moritz von
Engelhardt (*Ibid.*, pp. 29–34).
2. In 1876 he founded (with his friend Emil Schürer) the *Theologische Literaturzeitung*, which is still one of the foremost critical
reviews of theological scholarship. (Harnack was its sole editor
from 1881 on and held this post for many years.) In 1881–82 he
began (in co-operation with his friend O. von Gebhardt) the publication of the series *Texte und Untersuchungen* which, in the
course of time, became a mine of information on the history of the
ancient church.

office and affixed his signature to the document of Harnack's appointment on 17 September 1888.

The objections of the churchmen were based chiefly on Harnack's *History of Dogma* (3 vols., 1886–1889; 4th ed., 1909). They consisted mainly of the following charges: (1) that he doubted the traditional views concerning the authorship of the Fourth Gospel, of the Letter to the Ephesians, and of the First Epistle of Peter; (2) that he was critical of miracles and, specifically, that he did not accept the conventional interpretation of Christ's Virgin Birth, Resurrection, and Ascension; and (3) that he denied the institution of the sacrament of baptism by Jesus. No attempt was made to refute these views on the basis of historical scholarship from which they were derived, only the irreconcilability of Harnack's views with the doctrinal authority of the church was stated.

All this cast a shadow upon Harnack's academic position. Indeed, it darkened his entire career. Even at this time, to be sure, Harnack was of the conviction that the gospel of Jesus Christ had nothing in common with the doctrinal authority exercised by an ecclesiastical hierarchy or by a bureau of church officials. But the church to which he belonged felt it necessary to maintain this very authority. He could, therefore, hardly avoid some kind of conflict with it. Nevertheless, it was a source of deep sorrow for him that, throughout his life, he was denied all official recognition by the church. He was not even given the right to examine his own pupils as they

entered into the service of the church. Yet, for many
years, he was the most influential theological teacher.[3]

Hundreds, nay, thousands of students who later became ministers gave him an enthusiastic hearing, and

3. As an example of his students' gratitude for Harnack's teaching, I quote here a passage from a letter of Karl Holl which he
addressed to Harnack after Holl had attended Harnack's seminar
in the winter semester of 1889–90. (Harnack later decisively determined Holl's career: In 1891 he made him his collaborator in
the edition of the Greek Fathers which he prepared under the
auspices of the Berlin Academy of Sciences; and, in 1906, he was
instrumental in having Holl appointed as his special colleague to
the second chair of church history in the University of Berlin. In
this position, Holl gradually achieved great scholarly fame). Holl
wrote (on 18 April 1890): "It may be a rather one-sided way of
looking at things . . . yet as highly as I certainly appreciate
what you showed us about the grave tasks and the strict methods
of scholarship, I count it a higher gain that . . . you awakened
in me a joyful eagerness for serving our church . . . In extending
to you my special thanks, I want to give expression to my actual
experience and my deepest conviction that through you I have become aware of the extent to which every service we render to our
church, either of a scholarly or a practical kind, is a holy service
which must be rendered by serious work without fear of or sur-
render to human authorities. I hope that I may demonstrate in the
course of my life that in these respects I have not for nothing been
your pupil" (Heinrich Karpp [ed.], *Karl Holl: Briefwechsel mit
Adolf von Harnack* [Tübingen, 1966], pp. 11 f.).
    This particular correspondence shows very impressively with
what deep human understanding Harnack was able to relate himself to his students and colleagues as a scholar and as a friend.
Holl was often inclined to take life as a grave task and even as a
heavy burden and he therefore often tended toward pessimism.
Harnack tried again and again to give him courage and to cut him
free from his depressions. He once wrote to Holl: "May you learn
to rid yourself of the virtuosity of condemning each fruit-tree
which God has planted for your benefit as a weeping willow"
(Karpp, *K. Holl*, p. 18).

scores of them were inspired by him to prepare themselves for theological professorships, which then became centers from which his views were spread to ever-widening circles. As a member of the theological faculty of Germany's most distinguished university, which was maintained and supported by the state and protected by it as to its academic freedom, Harnack made an incisive contribution to the training of the leaders of the Protestant Church. This church was united with the same state, yet it never invited him to take a seat at its councils, synods, or boards, and it never gave him any assurance that as a theological teacher he was one of its spokesmen. Thus Harnack could not but be deeply disappointed in his strong desire to serve the church.[4]

In a wider sense, he served it, of course, through his prolific authorship. Most of his more than sixteen hundred large and small writings were devoted to the study of the history of the church.[5] The New Testament, the Church Fathers, but also the Reformation and Protestantism furnished him the main themes.

Certain of his works have already become classics.

4. The only opportunity he had to satisfy this wish was given him through his membership in the "Evangelical-Social Congress" (one of the voluntary associations so distinctive of modern Protestantism), whose purpose it was, outside the official church but through a membership recruited from the ranks of church members, to give concrete expression to the Christian responsibility for the social-political order. Harnack was its president from 1903 to 1912.

5. Cf. Friedrich Smend, A. von Harnack: Verzeichnis seiner Schriften (Leipzig, 1931), which lists 1611 titles.

His *History of Dogma,* for example, will have a permanent place among the masterpieces of theological literature. Though it will be superseded in specific parts, it
will always be recognized as a most suggestive work of
historical interpretation, grandly conceived and executed with superior skill both as to style and content.[6] The
work on *The Mission and Expansion of Christianity during the First Three Centuries* (2 vols., 1902; 4th ed.,
1924) is almost of the same quality. His *History of Ancient Christian Literature* (3 vols., 1893–1904) laid the
foundation for all further critical studies in patristics.

Few works of modern theological literature have cre-
ated as much excitement and stirred up as much furor
as Harnack's *Wesen des Christentums* (*What Is Christianity?,* 1900; 15th ed., 1950). It is the transcript of a
student's stenograph of a course of lectures delivered to
students of all faculties in the winter semester 1899–
1900. Troeltsch[7] thought that it was representative of
all theological work based on historical thinking. It certainly has become generally regarded as the one book

6. One of Harnack's admirers, the French Jesuit scholar J. de
Ghellinck, wrote about it ("En marge de l'oeuvre de Harnack,"
Gregorianum 11 [1930], pp. 513 f.): "Everyone knows the three
volumes of his *Dogmengeschichte,* though it is perhaps correct to
say that more people talk about them than read them." (*Chacun
les connait bien qu'il soit peut-être exact de dire que les trois volumes de sa Dogmengeschichte ont trouvé moins d'hommes pour
les lire que pour en parler.*)
7. Cf. Ernst Troeltsch, "Was heisst 'Wesen des Christentums?,'"
Gesammelte Schriften, II (1913), p. 387: *Harnack's Schrift ist
gewissermassen das symbolische Buch für die historisierende
Richtung der Theologie.*

which more directly than any other represents so-called liberal Protestant theology.

Harnack continued to publish scholarly and popular writings throughout his life. His authorship extended over fifty-seven years, from 1873, when he published his dissertation on Gnosticism, to 1930, when his publications ended with an article on the name of Novatian. His first important scholarly work had been a prize essay on Marcion (unpublished) for which the University of Dorpat had given him a gold medal; his last significant book was devoted to an interpretation of the same heretical figure,[8] and it stirred up considerable excitement.

In his capacity as an historian, Harnack was elected, in 1890, to the Prussian Academy of Sciences in Berlin. Theodore Mommsen, one of its most distinguished members, gave him an enthusiastic welcome. Here he soon became the organizer and chairman of the editorial council of the *Critical Edition of the Greek Christian Authors of the First Three Centuries*. Futhermore, he learned to relate theological scholarship to that of other disciplines. It was a signal honor that he, the theologian, was invited by the Academy to prepare its history which was to be published in connection with the celebration of its two hundredth anniversary in 1900. Harnack punctually fulfilled the assignment. In three volumes, he offered not only an interpretation of the activi-

8. *Marcion: Das Evangelium vom fremden Gott* (Berlin, 1921; 2nd ed., Leipzig, 1924).

ties of the Academy but, in connection with it, also a
history of modern scholarship.

At the dawn of the new century, he was at the height
of his career. When the anniversary of the Berlin Academy was celebrated in a glittering ceremony, he was the
official orator. It so happened that, just then, he occu-
pied also the post of rector of the University of Berlin.
Moreover, at this time his fame was spreading throughout the world in connection with the publication of the
book *What Is Christianity?* He wielded great influence
on educational affairs through the office of the Minister
of Education who frequently sought his counsel.[9] Ever
increasingly he became a representative personage. The
public saw in him scholarship personified. William II,
the German emperor, gave him special recognition, first
by inviting him into his company and then by bestow-
ing special honors upon him.[10]

All this had an effect upon his academic career. To be
sure, church historical teaching and research continued
to be his primary love and labor. But, in the course of
time, he came to assume two further professional responsibilities. Indeed, he said of himself that he was active in three different careers. In 1906 he accepted the
appointment to the post of Director General of the
Royal Library[11] in Berlin, the largest and most impor-

9. There was a certain time when the rumor was current that he
would be appointed Minister of Education.
10. He raised him to the dignity of hereditary nobility. Harnack
was the last scholar so honored in royal Prussia.
11. After World War I, it was called the Prussian State Library.

tant library in Germany. Some of his friends were disturbed; they feared that he might gradually abandon his theological career. But Harnack wrote to his friend, Professor Martin Rade in Marburg:

You come to know the world only insofar as you influence it. My new position will not make me a librarian so much as an organizer. I hope that my friends will find that theology is not made the loser thereby but that all branches of learning, including theology, will make a gain. I have *done* little in my life, and I should like, in a modest way, to supplement my work of lecturing and writing by a "doing" from which the whole community can profit. The church has not offered me an opportunity of this kind, and if such work were offered to me now, it would come too late for me.[12]

12. Agnes von Zahn-Harnack, *Adolf von Harnack*, 2nd ed. (Berlin, 1951), p. 325. See the very interesting and informative article by Felix E. Hirsch, "The Scholar as Librarian. To the Memory of Adolf von Harnack," in *The Library Quarterly* IX (1939), pp. 299–320. Hirsch describes in detail how imaginatively and effectively Harnack administered his new post, finding willing collaborators among the professional librarians, especially in the person of his first director, Paul Schwenke. He also reports with admiration as follows (p. 307): "The sums he was able to procure were astounding. The Prussian bureaucracy made concessions to him which would have seemed unbelievable [under his predecessor] and which they would have denied to any librarian not invested with Harnack's authority as a scholar . . . Although there was a strong upward trend in the financial resources of all the great libraries in the country, so rapid an increase in the budget figures as took place in the Royal Library was unparalleled. Shortly after Harnack had taken office, he persuaded the ministry to grant an extraordinary sum of 350.000 marks for the purchase of Prince Chigi's book collection and when that project had miscarried, he was permitted to spend the whole amount in filling gaps in the collections of the Royal Library . . . Harnack did not

He proved to be an excellent organizer and a brilliant administrator. Hence nobody was much surprised when in 1911 he accepted also the post of president of the *Kaiser Wilhelm Gesellschaft*.[13] This was a foundation organized (in connection with the celebration of the centennial of the University of Berlin and sponsored by the German Emperor) for the purpose of launching scientific research institutes in which scholars would pursue basic and applied research of a kind which the universities could not afford to become engaged in, on account of their primary responsibility for teaching and professional training. Under Harnack's leadership and with the support of government and industry, the foundation rapidly established several research institutes chiefly in the natural and medical sciences. Almost immediately they won world-wide recognition and influence.

Harnack continued to be president of the *Kaiser Wilhelm Gesellschaft* until the end of his life. He led its affairs when it assumed broader and poignantly practical responsibilities during World War I, and he saw it through the turmoil caused by Germany's military defeat and through the ensuing period of monetary inflation and economic depression. In the spring of 1930,

rest until he had increased the ordinary book budget from about 150.000 marks in 1905 to 316.000 marks in 1913." From the time of his appointment until his retirement at the age of 68, he paid a daily visit to the library. He came generally at noon and spent one and a half or two hours there!
13. Now called *Max Planck Gesellschaft*.

these duties led him to Heidelberg, where a new institute of medical research was to be opened. There he died, after a brief illness, on 10 June 1930.

In 1921 he had become a professor emeritus. He then gave up all administrative duties connected with his professorship and retired from the library, but he continued to teach (on a reduced schedule, of course) for several years.[14] In the spring of 1929, he delivered his last lecture in the University of Berlin and, at the same time, he closed his seminar on ancient church history over which he had presided continuously for one hundred and eight academic semesters. It always had been the center of his work and the headquarters of his professional labors. For in connection with the broad influence he exercised and throughout the deep impact that went forth from him to all fields of cultural endeavor, he always remained first of all a church historian and a theologian. Indeed, he embodied in his person a kind of cultural Protestantism, which was deeply anchored in his personal faith and reached out broadly upon the wide field of human civilization. "Creator of unforgettable scholarly works, a master of organization, he impressed everyone, wherever he appeared, as a dominating personality through clarity, sureness, and strength of will." [15]

14. In the fall of 1921, the German government offered him the post of ambassador to Washington, D. C., but he regretfully declined the honor.
15. Eduard Spranger, "Die Friedrich-Wilhelm-Universität in Berlin," in *Berliner Geist* (Tübingen, 1966), p. 49. Harnack was a

II

Whatever may have been the secret of Harnack's power and whatever was the source of his accomplishment as a scholar, administrator, public figure, and representative man, one can say that he was what he was and that he produced his great works in the way he did, because he was an unusually gifted teacher.

person of great charm. This is the impression one obtains from reading the biography which his daughter Agnes wrote with a rare and congenial understanding of her father (see note 12). It is also the testimony of all who knew him well. At the memorial service held at the University of Berlin, Professor Erich Seeberg spoke of "his dutiful discipline in so ordering his daily life and dividing his time that he was able to accomplish so much—coupled as this discipline was with a chivalrous and objective formality in his dealings with men and in the management of his relations with them" (Erich Seeberg, *Adolf von Harnack* [Tübingen, 1930], p. 25). At the same occasion the rector of the university, Professor Erhard Schmidt, a mathematician, characterized him as follows: "Harnack was of a noble, aristocratic character; his outward distinction was softened by a generous, considerate, and kind disposition. In conversation, he never let one feel his superiority; on the contrary, he enhanced the self-confidence of the one who was speaking with him by rearranging in a most agreeable way whatever was being said to him and putting it in such a form that the other took great delight in the thought he had expressed" (*Ibid.*, p. 6). From 1919 until 1930, the last year of his life, Harnack used to spend part of his vacations at Elmau in the Bavarian Alps, a famous "retreat" founded and led by Johannes Müller, a former theologian and a charismatic religious leader, who at that time exercised a profound influence upon German intellectuals by his fresh but utterly antitheological and undogmatic interpretation

One who was one of his students in Leipzig, at the very beginning of Harnack's career (in 1877–78), wrote almost fifty years later in the following enthusiastic way of the impression Harnack (who was then still in his twenties) made upon him and his fellow students:

We had the feeling that a new world was dawning upon us. We had been trained by capable teachers and we were taking courses from eminent professors and well-known scholars. But here we were touched by the aura of genius. Harnack combined in himself in a unique way the qualities required of a scholar with the gifts of a born teacher: concentrated inquisitiveness; tireless industry; the ability of ordering and forming his materials; a comprehensive memory; [16] critical astuteness; a clear and considered judgment,

of Jesus. (It was characteristic of Harnack that he felt at home in the community which this man inspired.) In a long essay written in memory of Harnack, Müller describes the latter's relation with others as follows: "He deeply enjoyed the rare opportunity to be able to talk with old and young as if he were one of them and undisturbed by his extraordinary position and his fame in the world. He felt himself particularly attracted to the feminine element, in view of the fact that generally he had to deal mainly with men. There he demonstrated the full nobility of an old culture and of Baltic aristocracy. But whether they were men, women, or girls, he entranced all who came in contact with him by the rare charm of his personality and he delighted them again and again by his captivating conversation. He was full of humor and he had an unlimited memory" (*Grüne Blätter* XXXLI [1930], p. 141).
16. Harnack's brother-in-law, H. Rassow, writes (*Christliche Welt* 44 (1930), p. 728): "I asked him once: 'How much time would you need in order to memorize one page of Greek that you had never seen before?' He replied: 'If I read the page slowly, I would know it by heart.'" The church historian Ernst Benz reports that when as a student he consulted Harnack, the latter

and, together with all this, a wonderful gift of intuition and combination and, at the same time, a marvelously simple, lucid, and appealing manner of presentation. And, to top it all, he also had not infrequently the good fortune of finding and discovering something new. To every subject and field of study he gave light and warmth, life and significance. In both theory and practice he was a master of the teaching method.

He came to his classes only after thorough preparation. He was never without notes, but he spoke extemporaneously . . . without affection or pathos and never seeking cheap effects. He talked eloquently and from an even inner participation in what he was dealing with, without trying to excite or overwhelm his hearers. Yet he was fascinating and convincing. He was illuminating through the gentle compulsion of complete objectivity. He was conscientious and accurate but not pedantic, nor did he get lost in details. Without minimizing or concealing difficulties, he explained the problems at hand with vividness as to their logical form and material content. He made the past live through the present and let the present explain the past.[17]

Many other testimonies prove that these striking words express the experience and judgment of the large circle of Harnack's students and pupils. Among these none is perhaps as telling as that of Dietrich Bon-

readily recited from memory entire passages from the writings of the Fathers and then confirmed his quotations by taking the relevant volumes from his shelves and finding the correct page at the first try. Cf. Ernst Benz, *Adolf v. Harnack zum 100. Geburtstag, Jahrbuch der Akademie der Wissenschaften und der Literatur in Mainz* (1952), p. 212.

17. *Christliche Welt* 35 (1921), p. 315. The writer was Professor W. Bornemann.

hoeffer,[18] who was a member of Harnack's last seminar
and who spoke in the name of his fellow students at the
memorial service on 15 June 1930 in Berlin. He said,
among other things:

He got hold of us in the way a real teacher gets hold of his
pupils. He shared our questions, even though he confronted
us with his superior judgment. We assembled in his home
for a serious piece of work on the history of the ancient
church, and there we came to know him and his unerring
striving for truth and clarity. All mere talk was foreign to
the spirit of his seminar. He demanded absolute clarity.
This did not exclude the possibility that very personal and
inmost questions were raised. He was always willing to
listen to questions and to answer them. All that mattered to
him was the honesty of the answer. Thus we learned from
him that truth is born only from freedom.[19]

We should note that as a teacher Harnack was an historian and that as an historian he was a teacher. The
role of the teacher is almost identical with that of the
historian. In a certain sense, every true teacher is an historian, and nobody can be a true historian unless he is
willing to be also a teacher. For, in every present, men
find that they must come to terms with the cultural legacy which they have inherited from their fathers. They
must take possession of it and incorporate it in their
own lives. They must fit it to the requirements of their

18. Bonhoeffer was executed because he opposed the Nazi dicta-
torship. Harnack's eldest son, Ernst, experienced the same fate.
19. *Adolf von Harnack: Ausgewählte Reden und Aufsätze* (Berlin, 1951), p. 210.

own situation and thus transform it and then transmit it
to their children and their children's children.

Civilization is a product of education and a learning
process at the same time. Men are engaged in it in order
to relate the values produced by past generations to the
needs of the present; at the same time, they endeavor to
hand them on to future generations. Whoever, therefore, furthers human culture is in a real sense a teacher
as well as an historian, for as he hands down the cultural traditions of the past to those around him, he acts
as an historically responsible educator.

In this sense, Harnack was a supreme teacher-his-
torian.[20] His writings as well as his activities clearly
prove that he believed it to be the highest task of the
historian to prepare his fellow men for right action in
the present.[21] "Only that history which is not yet past
but which is and remains a living part of our present
deserves to be known by all," he wrote.[22] Hence he regarded all history as mute as long as it is nothing but a
display of an antiquarian interest or dealt with only in
terms of archaeology, that is, as long as it is understood
to be merely a record of past human life.[23]

20. Cf. W. Pauck, "Harnack's Interpretation of Church History,"
The Heritage of the Reformation (Chicago, 1961), pp. 337 ff.
21. Cf. Hans Lietzmann, *Gedächtnisrede auf Harnack. Sitzungs-
berichte der Akademie der Wissenschaften in Berlin* (1931), p.
lviii.
22. In "Sokrates und die Alte Kirche," *Ausgewählte Reden und
Aufsätze* (1951), p. 25.
23. Cf. *Wesen des Christentums*, p. xvii, and *Reden und Aufsätze*, IV (Berlin, 1923), p. 5.

The following statement sums up Harnack's fundamental conception:

We study history in order to intervene in the course of history, and it is our right and duty that we do this, for if we lack historical insight we either permit ourselves to be mere objects put in the historical process or we shall have the tendency to lead people down the wrong way. To intervene in history—this means that we must reject the past when it reaches into the present only in order to block us. It means also that we must do the right thing in the present, that is, anticipate the future and be prepared for it in a circumspect manner. There is no doubt that, with respect to the past, the historian assumes the royal function of a judge, for in order to decide what of the past shall continue to be in effect and what must be done away with or transformed, the historian must judge like a king. Everything must be designed to furnish a preparation for the future, for only that discipline of learning has a right to exist which lays the foundation for what is to be.[24]

We should misunderstand the import of these words if we should take them to imply that Harnack was not concerned about the objectivity of historical research. He was wont to say that he was doing his work as an historian on three levels, namely, source criticism, representation, and reflection, and that he felt most at home on the third level.[25] And it is a fact that he de-

24. "Über die Sicherheit und Grenzen geschichtlicher Erkenntnis," *Reden und Aufsätze*, IV, 7.
25. The remark is reported by Walter Koehler; cf. *Theologische Blätter* 7 (1930), p. 168. Harnack wrote to K. Holl: "There is always the danger that one loses touch with general scholarship

voted much rigorous and time-consuming effort to the
establishment of the accuracy and reliability of his
sources, and, moreover, that he took great care to represent and interpret these sources as diligently and objectively as possible. But he was also painfully aware of
the limits that are set to the historian as he attempts to
reconstruct, to relate, and to interpret past actions and
events. He shared to some extent the skeptical judgment
of Goethe who is reported to have said in a conversation
with the historian Heinrich Luden: "Not all that is presented to us as history has really happened; and what
really happened did not actually happen the way it is
presented to us; moreover, what really happened is only
a small part of all that happened. Everything in history
remains uncertain, the largest event as well as the small-
est occurrence." [26]

As an historian, Harnack therefore did not try to tell
wie es eigentlich gewesen (what really happened), and,
indeed, he avoided all biographical history because he
suspected that it represented, especially in regard of
motivations, a necessarily unsuccessful engagement
with insoluble puzzles and inscrutable enigmas. Instead,

(mit der Wissenschaft im Grossen) when one works intensively
on one point, but it is of greater import to lose touch with special
scholarship (mit der Wissenschaft im *Kleinen*)."
26. Cf. his lecture on "Die Religion Goethes in der Epoche seiner
Vollendung," *Reden und Aufsätze*, IV, 157. It is important to
note here that, throughout his life, but particularly in his later
years, Harnack had a deep spiritual attachment to Goethe. In him
and his work, he saw the embodiment of the humanism of Western Christian civilization.

he chose to study the development of institutions, that is, states, societies, groups, and corporations and their established practices, customs, laws, codes, and authoritative rules. He interpreted institutional history as a history of ideas, for he judged that one cannot understand the development and the power of institutions unless one knows the direction along which they are moved by the ideas that govern and maintain them. For example, he believed it to be the historian's task to show to what extent an institution has succeeded in incorporating the idea or purpose for the concrete expression of which it was founded or in what way an institution may be striving to maintain itself even after it has lost the right to exist because the purpose which called it into being has become invalid or lost its directive power. He even dared define the norm by reference to which the historian can judge what institution or institutional function deserves to be maintained: that in them which preserves life. And he was persuaded that "only that line of action and that power preserve life which liberate men from 'the service to that which passes away,' from enslavement to mere nature, and from servitude to one's own empirical self." [27]

27. Cf. his lecture entitled: "Was hat die Historie an fester Erkenntnis zur Deutung des Weltgeschehens zu bieten?" in *Ausgewählte Reden und Aufsätze* (1951), p. 192.

III

Among Harnack's books, the *History of Dogma* is the
clearest expression of this basic conception of the historian's task. It shows concretely how and to what extent he tried to carry out his historical principles in his
own field of study. He himself describes the importance
of his interpretation of the history of dogma in the following way:

By delineating the process of the origin and development of
the dogma, the "history of dogma" furnishes the most suit-
able means for the liberation of the church from dogmatic
Christianity and for the speeding up of the irresistible process
of the emancipation which began with Augustine. But it
also witnesses to the unity of the Christian faith in the
course of history by furnishing proof that the actual significance of the person of Jesus Christ and the principles of
the gospel were never lost sight of.[28]

In writing the history of dogma, that is, the history of
those authoritative ecclesiastical doctrines concerning
the person and work of Christ, God incarnate, which
every Christian had to accept on peril of being excluded
from the communion of salvation, Harnack desired to
show, in the first place, how it happened that the gospel
of Jesus Christ, which in its nature has nothing in com-

28. Cf. *Grundriss der Dogmengeschichte,* 9th ed. (Berlin, 1921),
p. 5.

mon with ecclesiasticism and with authoritarian statutes
and doctrines, became embodied in the cultic-hierar-
chical practices and, especially, the doctrinal institutions of the church. But, in the second place, he wanted
to offer proof, by historical analysis, for the thesis that if
the gospel is to retain its living power today, it must be
freed from identification with the dogma. Indeed, it was
his major point that the dogma originated in the effort
of the ancient Christians to render the gospel comprehensible in the concepts of the Hellenistic world view
and that they therefore expressed it in the thought-
forms of Greek philosophy and science. Then he drew
the conclusion that, after having been maintained for
centuries through the doctrinal authoritarianism of the
church, the dogma has been coming to an end in the
way the various Christian churches and groups have
come to deal with it: In Eastern Orthodoxy it has become an uncomprehended relic kept alive only in the
cultus and the liturgy; in Roman Catholicism it has
become submerged in the hierarchical-sacramental order
of the church culminating in the absolute authority of
the Pope; the Reformation invalidated it in principle by
the rediscovery of the gospel and by the assertion of its
primacy in all Christian thought and life. However, the
reformers failed to recognize the full revolutionary significance of this rediscovery: instead of making room in
all Christian thought for the gospel alone, as they said it
was their purpose, they coupled the reformation of the

church on the basis of the gospel with the conservation of the dogma, in the interest, so they believed, of a scriptural catholicity. Thus it came about that the churches of the Reformation, namely, Lutheranism, Calvinism, and Anglicanism, exhibit in their orders and practices a personal faith in Christ in the context of authoritarian churchmanship. They have always required of the faithful obedient submission to the authority of ministers and ecclesiastical officials, and these are duty-bound to maintain conformity with the dogma.

It was Harnack's conviction that the Reformation must go on. Inasmuch as "every really important reformation in the history of religion was primarily a critical reduction," [29] Luther's rediscovery of the gospel must be completed by the emancipation of Christianity from doctrinal authoritarianism. He believed that the Hellenization of the gospel, which began with the formulation of the Logos-Christology and culminated in the promulgation of the Nicene dogma of the Trinity and of the Chalcedonian dogma of Christ, very God and very man, was an historical decision through which the Christian church succeeded in maintaining its identity in its confrontation with Hellenistic civilization and the Roman Empire; but he was also convinced that this Hellenization need not be continued forever, especially if this perpetuation can be accomplished only through an authoritarianism and an intellectual servitude which are irreconcilable with the gospel and its spirit. Having

29. *Wesen des Christentums*, p. 160.

in mind Luther and the Reformation, he summed up his basic view in the following words:

Christianity is something else than the sum of doctrines handed down from generation to generation. Christianity is not identical with biblical theology nor with the doctrine of the church-councils but it is that disposition which the Father of Jesus Christ awakens in men's hearts through the gospel. All authorities on which the dogma is based are torn down—how then can the dogma possibly be maintained as an infallible teaching! Christian doctrine is relevant only to faith; what part can philosophy then have in it? But what are dogma and dogmatic Christianity without philosophy? [30]

He concluded by asking: "How can there possibly be a history of dogma in Protestantism in view of Luther's 'Prefaces to the New Testament' and in view of his writings on the principles of the Reformation?" [31]

And with respect to the various historical forms which Christianity assumed in the course of time, beginning with the so-called Jewish Christianity of the Apostolic Age, he wrote: "Either Christianity is . . . identical with its first form (in this case, one is forced to conclude that it came and went at a certain time) or it contains something which remains valid in historically changing forms. Starting with the beginnings, church history shows that it was necessary for 'early Christianity' to perish in order that 'Christianity' might remain.

30. *Dogmengeschichte*, 4th ed., III, 896 f.
31. *Ibid.*, p. 898.

So too, there followed, later on, one metamorphosis upon another." [32]

We must acknowledge that this interpretation is thoroughly historical. By combining historical exposition with historical criticism, Harnack drew the full consequences from the application of the historical method to the Christian religion. In fact, he replaced the dogmatic method, which had been employed for so long a time in Christian thought, by the historical method. In doing so, he brought to a culmination the approach which had first been introduced into Christian theology by the historical theologians of the Enlightenment, especially Johann Salomo Semler (d. 1791), and which then resulted in the interpretation of Christianity as a "development" at the hands of Ferdinand Christian Baur (d. 1860) and Albrecht Ritschl (d. 1889), whom Harnack regarded as his immediate predecessors. [33] He relied on the work of these historical theologians and brought it to a climax

32. *Wesen des Christentums*, p. xix. Cf. *Dogmengeschichte*, 4th ed., I, 85: "The church historian is duty-bound not to be satisfied with the establishment of the fact that the Christian religion underwent changes but to examine to what extent new forms of it were able to protect, to implant, and to instill the gospel. In all probability the gospel would have perished if the form of 'early Christianity' had been preserved in the church; but, as a matter of fact, early Christianity perished in order that the gospel might prevail."
33. Cf. the recent and highly informative books: Philip Hefner, *Faith and the Vitalities of History: A Theological Study Based on the Work of Albrecht Ritschl* (New York, 1965); and Peter C. Hodgson, *The Formation of Historical Theology: A Study of Ferdinand Ch. Baur* (New York, 1966).

insofar as, in following out the implications of the historical method, he substituted for the traditional dogmatic norm of Christian theological truth the historical concept of the nature of Christianity (*Wesen des Christentums*). Thus he hoped to replace theological dogmatism by historical understanding.

In the introduction to a new edition of his lectures on the nature of Christianity, he wrote: "Historical understanding is achieved only as one makes the effort of separating the distinctive essence of an important phenomenon from the temporary historical forms in which it is clothed." [34] In these lectures, which constitute a summary and a popularization of the results of his scholarly investigations, he tried to achieve this understanding by identifying the nature of Christianity with the gospel and its influences. He therefore dealt first with the gospel of Jesus Christ, then with the impact which Jesus himself and his gospel made upon the first generation of his disciples, and finally with the main types of the Christian religion as they developed from the changes which it underwent in its encounter with different human conditions. He proposed to discover what these movements had in common by testing them by the gospel. Furthermore, he believed that he would be able to define the principles (*Grundzüge*), that is, the main characteristics of the gospel, by verifying them through a study of the various ways by which the gospel was understood in the course of church history.

34. *Wesen des Christentums*, p. xix.

It is often said that Harnack identified the nature of
Christianity with the teachings of Jesus. But this is an
undiscriminating simplification of his view. He did not
think it possible, it is true, to define the Christian religion apart from the gospel of Jesus Christ, but he did
not isolate this gospel from its historical impact, nor did
he absolutize it on the basis of the New Testament
where it is recorded in its earliest form. No historical
form of Christianity, he believed, should be absolutized
or regarded as normative.[35] "One may say," he wrote,
"that Paul or Augustine or Luther were right [in their
conception of the Christian gospel], yet one must never
go so far as to regard their Christianity as Christianity
itself." [36] He was persuaded that wherever the gospel of
Jesus Christ is actually believed, that is, where it is
really apprehended by way of a commitment to God derived from faith in this gospel (so that this commitment
is a certain trustful disposition of the heart), there
Christianity is realized: the impulse which motivates
such an actualization, and the fountain which feeds it is
the gospel—the gospel which Jesus proclaimed and of
which he was the concretion in his historical humanity.

Harnack never stated in so many words what he conceived the nature of Christianity to be (and we should
realize that no historian would attempt to offer a final

35. *Wesen des Christentums*, p. 113: "The gospel did not enter
the world as a statutory religion and it can therefore have no classical and permanent manifestation in any form of intellectual or
social expression, not even in the first one."
36. *Ibid.*, p. xviii.

definition), but he undertook again and again the task of defining the gospel. We must take care not to isolate certain ones of these definitions from the rest lest we illegitimately distort his thought.

He loved to quote Luther's saying, supposedly under the assumption that it summarized the gospel: "In forgiveness of sins there is life and bliss." Or he said: "The religion of the gospel rests upon . . . faith in Jesus Christ, i.e., because of him, this particular historical person, the believer is certain that God rules heaven and earth and that God the Judge is also the Father and Redeemer." [37] In the *History of Dogma*, he asserted that the gospel as the New Testament presents it is something twofold: [38] (1) the preaching of Jesus, and (2) the proclamation of Jesus as the Christ who died and rose again for the sake of sin and who gives the assurance of forgiveness and eternal life.

Many, therefore, misunderstand Harnack when they hold that he thought that the gospel consists ultimately only of the teaching of Jesus. There is, of course, no denying that he put great stress upon the teaching of Jesus. Indeed, he has become famous for the definition he offers in *What Is Christianity?* In the teaching of Jesus, he says there,[39] there are three circles of thought, each of which contains the whole proclamation: (1) the Kingdom of God and its coming; (2) God the Father

37. *Dogmengeschichte*, 4th ed., I, 70.
38. *Ibid.*, pp. 65 ff.
39. *Wesen des Christentums*, p. 31.

and the infinite value of the human soul; (3) the better
righteousness and the commandment of love. He was
concerned to emphasize that this teaching must be received with full seriousness. For he was persuaded that
it was not something merely provisional which must be
differently understood in the light of Jesus' death and
resurrection,[40] as if only a certain conception of the
person of Christ (for example, that he was the "Son of
God," etc.) could ensure the proper comprehension of
the gospel.

"Not the Son but alone the Father belongs in the gospel as Jesus proclaimed it." [41] By saying this, Harnack
in no way intended to minimize the significance of
Jesus. He wanted only to make sure that the gospel was
understood as a religious-moral proclamation addressed
to man's conscience which requires from him a decision
for or against it and will then bring about a transforma-
tion of his inner disposition. He desired thus to avoid
the impression that the gospel must be taken to be a
revelation of an extraordinary sort which can be maintained only on the basis of certain metaphysical views
about God, Christ,[42] man, and the world. He felt it

40. *Ibid.*, p. 86.
41. *Ibid.*
42. Cf. *ibid.*, p. 122: "For most of us this identification [of the
Messiah with the Logos] is unacceptable because our thinking
about the world and about ethics does not lead us to conclude
upon a logos as being (*einen wesenhaften Logos*). To be sure, the
affirmation 'the Logos has appeared among us' had an exciting
effect, but the enthusiasm and the rapture of soul which it evoked
did not lead with certainty to the God whom Jesus proclaimed."

necessary to insist on saying that "Jesus does not belong
to the gospel as one of its elements," [43] for, in fact, he
thought of him as highly as possible.

He was the personal concretion and power of the gospel,
and we still perceive him as such. For none has ever known
the Father in the way he knew him, and he gives this
knowledge to others, thereby rendering "the many" an in-
comparable service. He leads them to God, not only by his
word but still more by what he is and does and, finally, by
his suffering. It is in this sense that he said not only this:
"Come unto me all ye that labor and are heavy laden and
I will give you rest," but also this: "The Son of Man is not
come to be ministered unto but to minister and give his
life as a ransom for many." [44]

Throughout his life, Harnack was certain that because of this gospel, Christianity was *the* true religion.
"It is *the* religion," he wrote,[45] "because Jesus Christ is
not one among other masters but *the* master and because his gospel corresponds to the innate capacity of
man as history discloses it."

In order to do full justice to Harnack's basic conception, we must note also that he frequently pointed out
what the gospel and the Christian religion are not. "The
Christian religion is something lofty and simple and is
concerned only about one point: Eternal life in the
midst of time through God's power and in his presence.

43. *Ibid.*, p. 87.
44. *Ibid.*
45. "Die Aufgabe der theologischen Fakultäten und die allge-
meine Religionsgeschichte," *Reden und Aufsätze*, II (Giessen,
1910), p. 172 f.

It is not an ethical or social arcanum for the purpose of preserving all sorts of things or of improving them. Even the mere question of what it has contributed to the cultural progress of mankind does harm to its spirit." [46] It is an error, therefore, to apply the gospel directly to secular affairs and to deduce from it detailed prescriptions and statutes for their regulation.[47] It is something religious; indeed, it is religion itself and as such a disposition of mind marked by worship in spirit and in truth. Hence it cannot and must not be expressed in laws and regulations or in a worship through signs, liturgical rituals, and idols.[48] Its true nature is threatened if it is linked with or confined to authoritative forms of faith and order, dogma and liturgy, law and hierarchy. Ecclesiasticism, so Harnack affirmed,[49] frequently imposed a terrible burden upon the gospel but it never succeeded in suppressing its power. However, the most momentous conformity which, he thought, ecclesiastical authority has been wont to require and still requires of Christians is the doctrinal one. This is detrimental to the gospel, not because of doctrine as such (though the gospel is not a doctrine!), but because of the fact that, from the beginning, Christian dogmatic thought was combined with Greek philosophy of religion and with the intellectualism characteristic of this philosophy. The result was not only that the Christian

46. *Wesen des Christentums*, p. 5.
47. *Ibid.*, pp. 38, 71.
48. *Ibid.*, p. 141.
49. *Ibid.*, p. 158; *Dogmengeschichte*, 4th ed., I, 82.

faith came to be dependent upon metaphysics but also
—and this was an observation which Harnack thought
was amazing and shocking—that a "fancied Christ was
put in the place of the real one." [50]

IV

These several points are an indication of the program
which Harnack advocated (explicitly and implicitly)
for Christianity in the modern world. In conclusion, we
now direct our attention to his major programmatic
convictions and recommendations.

We must give priority to a concern which runs
through his entire theological work, namely, that Christians should be freed from the requirement of holding
certain rigidly defined doctrines and of maintaining
other traditions only because they are regarded as authoritative in connection with a dogma whose absolute
validity is simply taken for granted or affirmed without
question. During the negotiations about his call to the
University of Berlin, he addressed a memorandum to
the Minister of Education [51] in which he made the following declaration: "Neither exegesis nor dogmatics but
the results of church historical research will break the
power of the traditions which are now burdening the

50. *Wesen des Christentums,* p. 140.
51. 27 November 1888. Agnes von Zahn-Harnack, *Adolf von
Harnack,* 130f.

consciences of men. Cardinal Manning once made the
following frivolous statement: 'One must overcome history by dogma'—we say just the opposite; dogma must
be purified by history. As Protestants we are confident
that by doing this we do not break down but build up."

Harnack's whole theological work can be regarded as
a commentary on this statement. He wanted to see authoritarian dogmatic thinking replaced by historical
thinking. He knew how difficult it would be to achieve
this goal. For he was aware of the fact that "there is
nothing more conservative and unyielding than ordered
religion." [52] Indeed, he had the greatest respect for the
Roman Catholic Church because it had succeeded in
maintaining itself throughout many ages by means of
this conservatism. "The Roman Church," he said, "is the
most comprehensive and powerful, the most complex
and yet most uniform structure which known history
has produced." [53]

In order to liberate the gospel from the connection
with this powerful institution, Harnack believed that
the reformers had to renounce in some way the Roman
Catholic ideal of building a visible Kingdom of God on
earth and of penetrating the realm of nature with the
power of grace and holiness, but in order to return the
Christian religion to its spiritual core, they had no
choice but to effect a tremendous reduction.[54] The re-

52. *Wesen des Christentums,* p. 104.
53. *Ibid.,* p. 166.
54. *Reden und Aufsätze,* IV, 338 (in an address in commemora-
tion of A. Ritschl).

sult was that the gospel was once more clearly seen in distinction from Roman ecclesiasticism. However, the reformers did not go far enough. They abolished Roman ecclesiasticism in the name of the Word of God and they assailed its foundations but they left the dogma intact. Luther had a certain historical sense and, to some extent, was able to apply historical criticism to purely dogmatic authority. For example, he rejected the notion of the infallible authority of the Papacy by pointing out that it was the product of changing history. But his thinking was not really determined by historical sense.[55] Hence he was unable to recognize the Scripture as an historical product. For the same reason, he argued that the dogma declared by the ancient councils of the church was valid inasmuch as it agreed with the Word of God. The other reformers, with the exception of a few humanistic representatives of the left wing of the Reformation, followed in Luther's train. Hence, so Harnack concluded, "Protestantism was unable, from the beginning, to develop fully, consistently, and strongly. It continued to be heavily burdened with Catholic remnants. When the Enlightenment finally came to its assistance, it brought with it a certain unproductive self-sufficiency which spoiled everything. Because of this, it failed to recognize the historical element through which faith in God the Father is linked with Jesus Christ." [56]

Modern historical theology must complete what the

55. *Dogmengeschichte*, 4th ed., III, 867.
56. *Ibid.*, p. 906.

Reformation began—this was Harnack's program. The application of historical thinking to all parts and phases of the Christian religion would make it possible, he believed, for the gospel of Jesus Christ to run a free, unhindered course in the world. "It must become possible," he wrote, "that one may openly say that such and such teachings and affirmations of the creeds are incorrect and that nobody is forced to confess in the Divine Service what once he is outside he does not need to confess." [57]

He hoped that the time would come when traditional dogmatic Christianity would be replaced by an undogmatic Christianity.[58] At the end of his life, he stated

57. Agnes von Zahn-Harnack, *Adolf von Harnack,* p. 315.
58. In this connection, it is interesting to note that throughout his career, Harnack found himself unable to regard systematic or dogmatic theology with the same seriousness which the "dogmatists" were accustomed to demand for it from themselves and others. For example, Theophil Wurm, later bishop of Württemberg and widely known as a prominent opponent of Hitler, reports that Harnack said in the course of a seminar which Wurm, then a student, attended in 1894 (cf. *Theologische Blätter* 9 [1930], p. 273), that he would propose the following outline to anyone wishing to write a dogmatic theology: "Part I: The teachings of Jesus and the apostolic interpretation of them. Part II: Mysteries; in this part, he added, one could proceed to speculate as much as one liked." And Karl Barth writes (*Kirchliche Dogmatik* I; II [1938], pp. 403f.) that in the last conversation they had together, Harnack told him that if he had to write a "dogmatics," he would entitle it: "The Life of God's Children." Barth goes on to explain that Harnack intended by this suggestion to propose the substitution of the traditional kind of dogmatic theology by the personal confession of a Christian who had achieved maturity by letting his thinking be centrally determined by the history of Christianity.

that he felt a certain kinship with the Congregational-
ists and the Quakers.[59] There can be no doubt that his
whole theological outlook was similar to that of the
"theologians" of the American denominations which
represent the so-called free-church tradition.

There are three great themes to which he returned
again and again in connection with his advocacy of the
undogmatic, historical thinking in religion and theology: (1) the canonical authority of the Old Testament;
(2) the doctrine of Christ; (3) the unity of Christendom.[60]

(1) In order to release Protestantism from the
shackles of literalistic biblicism and the dogmatics connected therewith, and in order to be consistent with the
historical interpretation of the Bible, indeed, in order
just to "honor the truth," Harnack felt that the Protestant churches should break with the tradition of treat-
ing the Old Testament as a book of *canonical authority*.
In his work on Marcion, he wrote (and he was then at
the end of his career): "In the second century, the re-
jection of the Old Testament would have been a mistake
and the Great Church rightly refused to make this mistake; its retention in the sixteenth century was due to
the power of a fateful heritage from which the reformers were not yet able to withdraw; but its conservation

59. Cf. his correspondence with Professor Erik Peterson, reprinted in the latter's *Theologische Traktate* (München, 1951), p.
258.
60. *Marcion: Das Evangelium vom fremden Gott*, 2nd ed., p.
217.

as a canonical book in modern Protestantism is the result of a paralysis of religion and the church." Harnack
did not mean, of course, to suggest that Christians, and
particularly the historians and theologians among them,
should no longer study the Old Testament. On the contrary, he thought that from the historical point of view
it would always not only be good and useful but also
necessary to read it in relation to the New Testament.
But he was convinced that only the New Testament was
the basic Christian book and that it alone, therefore,
should be held as Holy Scripture.

This view called forth a storm of protest, and it still
does. Harnack's critics felt that he was assailing the
very foundation of Christianity. Barth, for example, responded to Harnack's insistence that Protestantism
should "clearly decide" against the canonicity of the
Old Testament by saying: "In respect of this we merely
remark that if the Evangelical Church were to do this,
it would lose its identity with the Church of the first
seventeen centuries." [61] It is difficult to imagine that
this point would have greatly impressed Harnack, for
his whole proposal was inspired by the realization that,
in terms of historical reality, modern Protestantism is
not and cannot be "identical" with the church of former
ages.[62]

61. *Kirchliche Dogmatik* I; II, p. 82.
62. Agnes von Zahn-Harnack cites (*Adolf von Harnack,* pp.
244f.) a letter which her father wrote to Karl Holl with reference
to the discussion which his book on Marcion had elicited: "Is it
not so that the Ancient Church was not aware of the fact that

(2) Of much greater importance to Harnack was his hope that modern Christians would free themselves from the burden of the dogma about the person of Jesus. Even as late as 1925,[63] he said: "By combining all the various affirmations about Christ in the one confession and witness that he is the mirror of God's paternal heart,[64] one can get free from the entire ancient dogma and, at the same time, hold fast to the root of faith." He was sure that it is not possible for any man, on the basis of faith or knowledge, to make any valid statements about Christ's nature and particularly his "divine nature." Christians must be content with the New Testament and leave room for the same diversity of thought and speech which the early Christians displayed in relation to their understanding of the lordship of Christ.

Harnack looked forward with keen anticipation to the Lausanne Conference on Faith and Order in 1927. He hoped that there the churches would achieve some clarity about Christology. In a memorandum,[65] he expressed the opinion that the deliberations of the confer-

---

truth too develops? . . . I did not find it difficult to cause my children to accept the teaching that the Old Testament is now antiquated and only in certain parts still appealing and valuable. It is the law and history of the Jews; *our* book is the New Testament."

63. *Ibid.,* p. 161, in an address to the Evangelical-Social Congress.

64. This was a phrase of Luther's making (cf. his *Larger Catechism*). Harnack was very fond of it and used it frequently.

65. Agnes von Zahn-Harnack, *Adolf von Harnack,* pp. 420ff.

ence were "a fateful hour of decision for the Christian church" insofar as they would either make a contribution to clarification and unification of a sort the churches had not experienced for centuries or increase the division of Christendom. Then he went on to say:

There is a significant consensus in Christology. No one denies either the uniqueness or the unity of the person of the Redeemer; nor does anyone deny that the Christian faith is faith in the Father, the Son, and the Holy Spirit and that its universal confession is that in Jesus Christ the Word became flesh . . . Should we not be satisfied with this consensus as it is expressed in the confessional affirmations that Christ is the "Son of God," the "God-Man," the "Image of God," "Our Lord"? In my judgment, this should be sufficient, and the churches would leave it to every Christian how he might further conceive the person of Christ. But, as a matter of fact, this consensus is not sufficient in our day; we need a formal decision, for, at the great ancient councils, the churches have ordained that one must believe in the *two natures* of Christ and that any statement about him in which this speculation about his two natures is rejected must be considered heretical . . . But, in the course of the last two centuries, numerous Christians have found it impossible to express the faith in Christ through the speculation about the two natures, etc. . . . The Conference on Faith and Order will have to decide whether it shall demand that the dogmatic affirmation: Christ had two natures, shall continue to be an affirmation of faith or whether it is prepared to reaffirm the faith in the Father, the Son, and the Holy Spirit and, therefore, also in the God-man Christ, but, as far as the churches are concerned, to make no binding rules about any further speculation.

This expectation of Harnack was not fulfilled and has not been fulfilled to this day. No church body has ever officially renounced or given up or modified any dogmatic decision made by the official bodies of the ancient church.

(3) Harnack ardently believed in Christian unity. He was convinced that the Christian religion was the greatest force for the reconciliation of men with one another. He experienced with gratification the awakening of the ecumenical movement and entertained great hopes for it. But he felt strongly that such unity could be brought about only if all intolerance based on dogmatism and doctrinal authoritarianism were banished from the life of the churches.

V

After World War I, the fashion of theological thinking changed radically. The leadership of Harnack, the historian, was replaced by that of Karl Barth, the dogmatist. The difference between them as to theological method was so great that Harnack, who was one of Barth's teachers, found himself utterly unable to follow Barth. "He was ready to acknowledge Barth's deep seriousness, but his theology made him shudder." [66]

Barth has explained the difference between his own outlook and that of Harnack by pointing to the fact

66. Agnes von Zahn-Harnack, *Adolf von Harnack*, p. 415.

that, following Schleiermacher, all "modern" Protestant theologians pursued their work by proceeding *von unten nach oben* (from man to God), whereas he advocates a method which goes *von oben nach unten* (from God to man). There is much truth in this distinction. And saying this does not necessarily mean that truth is on Barth's side. He begins his theological interpretation with revelation, and God's revelation remains his theme throughout. But the question is, by what right he can begin and proceed in this way. For he is a man and as such he is bound to history; he should therefore be ready (but he is not!) to admit that like all other knowledge also the knowledge of God can be available to him only historically.

Harnack, by contrast, started with the assumption that, together with everything else that belongs to man's realm, the Christian religion is something historical, a heritage with which every generation has to deal with respect to the past as well as to the future. Is then truth not on his side insofar as he insisted that the only adequate method of dealing with Christianity is the historical one? The discussion of this question will occupy theology for many years to come, and in this discussion Harnack's views will continue to be important.

Ernst Troeltsch

I

It is more than forty-five years since Troeltsch died at the height of his career, but his influence is still strong and his powerful personality remains unforgotten. Despite the fact that his work as a theologian has been greatly neglected under the impact of Karl Barth and his neo-orthodox followers, students and thinkers still turn to Troeltsch. In recent years, this has been happening more and more frequently. His books are again read, especially by those who want to understand the origin and character of modern civilization and the place of religion in it.

Paul Tillich was aware of the great intellectual debt he owed to Troeltsch. He remembered particularly what he had learned from him about the nature of history and about the problems of the theology of culture. Both Reinhold and H. Richard Niebuhr have often acknowledged that their ways of handling theological problems were deeply determined by their study of Troeltsch's writings. Reinhold Niebuhr has been a Troeltschian from the time when he published his first book, *Does Civilization Need Religion?* until these latter days when he wrote an addendum to all his studies on man's historical nature and destiny in the little book on *Man's Nature and His Communities.* His brother H. Richard, who was such an effective and influential teacher of theological ethics, wrote his doctoral dissertation on Ernst Troeltsch. All his books, but especially *The Social Sources of Denominationalism, Christ and Culture,* and *The Meaning of Revelation,* plainly show how his mind was shaped by Troeltsch's preoccupation with problems of ethics and society in Christian civilization. This is especially to be noted in view of the fact that, for a considerable time, he let his thinking be determined also by the theology of Karl Barth. Indeed, his thought was constituted by a kind of synthesis between Troeltsch and Barth, almost an "impossible possibility," because Troeltsch lacked an aerial for the Barthian methods of theological thinking just as Harnack did, and Barth, on his part, has frequently declared that, because, like Schleiermacher, Troeltsch saw in Christianity not a divine revelation but only a manifestation of religion, he was unable to do justice to the meaning of the gospel of Jesus Christ.

Many of the students of Reinhold and Richard Niebuhr probably do not know what they owe through their teachers to Troeltsch. However, all who have gone through the classrooms and seminars of James Luther Adams certainly have been made conscious of the high esteem in which this sociologist and historian of theology has held Troeltsch. He has absorbed the thought of Paul Tillich with more thoroughness than any one else has done in this country. When his translations and interpretations of Troeltsch are published, it will be seen to what extent he has appropriated for himself the latter's social and historical ethics; we shall also be able to note how he has responded to Troeltsch in contrast to Paul Tillich.

In recent years, a considerable number of doctoral theses about the work of Troeltsch have been written and published both in this country and abroad. What their final significance for theological and historical scholarship will be, remains to be seen. But one may safely assume that Troeltsch will not remain ineffective upon the minds of those who have studied him closely.

II

It was my good fortune to be a student in several of Troeltsch's courses at the University of Berlin in the years 1920 and 1921. Troeltsch lectured on the history of philosophy, on ethics in the context of cultural history, and on similar topics. These lectures will remain unforgettable to me, not only because of the ideas and insights which they communicated to me and not only because they gave me the impetus to turn to theology as a full-time student, but chiefly because of the impression upon me of the professor's personality. I am sure that most of the other students in these courses (there were

in each nearly one thousand) were as deeply affected as
I was.

Troeltsch was then a man in his middle fifties, of middle height, stocky and broad-shouldered. His hair and
his handle-bar moustache were gray. As he spoke, his
gray eyes shone brightly, and when he laughed, which
was often, he showed a set of beautifully regular teeth.
He spoke with great animation and he threw his whole
person into the act of speaking. He waved his arms and
pointed with his hands and stamped his feet. His hair,
which at the beginning of the lecture was carefully
combed, became quickly messed up. His eyeglasses, a
pair of pince-nez, which he needed in order to consult
his notes from time to time, continually fell from his
nose and then dangled from his vest to which they were
fastened by a black band. All the while, words fell from
his lips like a torrent, and they were powerfully effective. Troeltsch's eloquence held us fascinated and spell-
bound. It was irresistible. We hung on every word. He
spoke with a strong baritone voice in a curious rhythm.
He seldom repeated the same word, and his sentences
were quite long and involved. What he said was syn-
thetic rather than analytical or critical. He placed many
observations next to one another, referring all the while
to other thinkers and quoting them, and he pointed to
historical events, movements, and ideas. When he was
done with any part of his lecture, one saw clearly what
he had intended to convey.

There are similar testimonies to Troeltsch's oratorical power. One of the most impressive is that of the poet and novelist Gertrud von le Fort. She was a student of Troeltsch's in Heidelberg shortly before World War I. She later converted to Roman Catholicism but remained a friend of her teacher. In 1925 she published her lecture notes on Troeltsch's "Dogmatics." In one of her post-World War II novels, she set a moving monument to Troeltsch: He was the model of one of the main figures in her book *Der Kranz der Engel*.[1] She describes her reaction to Troeltsch's lecturing as follows: "It is impossible for me to report on the impressions this lecture made upon me, for it went above my head. Intellectually, I understood only very little. And yet the impact as such was overwhelming. For the first time in my life, I found myself exposed to and under the disturbing sway of the power of an enormous eloquence, the power of something elemental—say the power of the sea or of a storm—but yet very clearly with the distinctive awareness that this elemental power was the bearer or wing of something spiritual."[2]

Professor Georg Wünsch, who also was a student of Troeltsch in Heidelberg, says something similar: "He lectured in such a colorful, captivating way that one's

1. See the remark of A. Dietrich at the conclusion of his brief biography of Troeltsch in *Biographisches Jahrbuch, 1923* (Berlin, 1930), pp. 349–368.
2. G. von le Fort, *Der Kranz der Engel*, 6th ed. (Munich, 1953), p. 80.

breath stood still. Only the sound of the bell recalled
one to the consciousness of one's own self." [3]

His manner of writing was similar to that of his
speaking. His books therefore have an effect upon the
readers which is very similar to that which his lectures
had upon those who heard them.

At the time when I sat in his courses (and this was in
the years immediately after the First World War), he
was much too busy to be able to enter into a personal
relationship with his students. He was then active in
politics as one of the founders of the new Democratic
Party. He served for a time as an Undersecretary of
State in the Ministry of Education and Public Worship,
and in this capacity, he exercised considerable influence
upon the definitions of the rights and functions of
schools and churches which were ultimately included in
the constitution of the Weimar Republic. He was then
also at the height of his academic fame and much
sought after as a lecturer and commentator on public
events. He was thus not easily accessible to us.

Perhaps this corresponded to his character. He certainly was outgoing, communicative, and friendly. But,
at the same time, he gave the impression of one who
preferred not to become very personal in his relations
with others. There was something about him that be-
trayed reserve and even shyness.

Here are two remarkable descriptions of his personal

3. "Ernst Troeltsch zum Gedächtnis," *Christliche Welt* 37 (1923),
p. 105.

character. Professor Heinrich Hofmann, one of Troeltsch's pupils and later for many years a professor in the University of Bern, Switzerland, wrote about him as follows:

He was of an effervescent temperament and his speech poured forth like a cataract. How impetuous could he be and what drastically direct words could he form when he was engaged in polemics; how heartily he could laugh when, because of his views, a certain number of whigs again became wobbly. Yet in this powerful nature there lived an inward tenderness; his explosive power was inwardly checked by a deep ethos, by measured restraint and human considerateness. It was this combination of power and moderation which constituted the charm of his personality.[4]

In the later years of his life, one of Troeltsch's closest friends was the historian Friedrich Meinecke. They were both intensely interested in the problems of the philosophy of history and they were of the same mind in their judgment of political affairs. Meinecke wrote several highly informative and deeply sympathetic essays about his friend. In one of them he speaks of him as follows:

One had to hear him talk in order to understand him fully. Then the lively and bold but energetically conceived abstract thought-complexes, which he liked quite cyclopedically to heap up in enormous sentence-structures, assumed at once an inner vitality and a fascinating clearness; then there appeared behind the great thinker a great human be-

4. Heinrich Hofmann, "Ernst Troeltsch zum Gedächtnis," *Theologische Blätter* 2 (1923), p. 77.

ing for whom all knowledge was transformed into personal-spiritual vitality. He was a God-seeker of the great manner who impetuously questioned and criticized the great God-seekers of world-history while, at the same time, he revered them. In every moment, he was both a sceptic and a believer; simultaneously analytical and constructive; in need of faith and thirsty for life.[5]

It is not easy to say much about him that is biographical. In his numerous writings, the references to his personal life and career are sparse. He certainly was no autobiographical thinker like Paul Tillich, although he could from time to time be quite frank in expressing his feelings and judgments about himself and others among his friends and critics. Moreover, he certainly was gifted with a remarkable skill of describing the character of men and movements. But he said very little about himself which is biographically substantial. The only self-description we have of him is an essay characteristically entitled "My Books" which he furnished to a symposium and which contains brief autobiographies written by distinguished professors of philosophy.[6] Only very few of his letters have ever been published. His literary remains, I understand, were destroyed in the bombing attacks upon Germany during World War II. What others have said or reported about him, particularly his friends at the time of his death, is, though generally brief, often

5. Friedrich Meinecke, "Zur Theorie und Philosophie der Geschichte" in *Werke*, IV (Stuttgart, 1959), p. 364.
6. Reprinted in the 4th volume of *Collected Works* (*Gesammelte Schriften*, IV [Berlin, 1925], p. 3–20).

quite revealing and informative. The following biographical sketch is based upon these incomplete
sources.

III

Ernst Troeltsch was born near Augsburg as the oldest
son of a physician on 17 February 1865. He was the de-
scendant of South-German burghers of Swabian and
Bavarian stock, and the "mild," that is, unaggressive,
nationalism which he displayed in his political activities
throughout his life was determined by this heritage. He
was educated at the Anna-Gymnasium in Augsburg.
There he received a thorough humanistic education in a
cultural setting which was strongly determined through
family, school, and pulpit by what was then called neo-
orthodox Lutheranism, a form of Lutheran churchmanship which permitted an orthodox confessionalism to
enter into an alliance with Pietism and Romanticism.[7]
He remained always grateful that he was given this
training "in wonderfully few prescribed courses and
hours of instruction." [8]

Troeltsch himself later wrote that "his drive for
knowledge was directed from the beginning toward the
world of history," [9] but his mind was always open for

7. Wünsch, *Christliche Welt* 37 (1923), p. 106,
8. *Gesammelte Schriften*, IV, 3.
9. *Ibid.*

the natural sciences, and thus he came to see at an early time all problems of history and of the philosophy of culture in the framework of a scientific world view. His father hoped that, at the proper time, he would take up the study of medicine, and he constantly stimulated his son's scientific interests. Troeltsch later remembered that in his parental house he always had the opportunity of observing and consulting "skeletons, anatomic charts, electrical machines, and botanical and geological collections and books." This was at the time when Darwinism first became popular among the educated throughout the Western world.

When, in 1884, Troeltsch entered the University of Erlangen, he found it difficult to decide what studies he should take up. The law attracted him only in connection with history insofar as it seemed to him to determine the great institutions which form the historical development. He was fascinated also by classical philology, but he thought that his teachers had demonstrated to him by their demeanor and outlook that the Greek ideals of life were no longer realizable. Philosophy did not appeal to him because it was not creative; and medicine interested him only theoretically. "Hence," he said, "I became a theologian." [10] He believed that theology furnished the most interesting themes for study because it appeared to him to raise fruitful metaphysical problems and at the same time get one involved in intense historical questions.

10. *Ibid.*, p. 4.

Yet, the theological faculty of Erlangen did not im-
press him. To be sure, several of its members, F. H. R.
Frank, K. A. G. von Zezschwitz, Th. Zahn, were influential and even famous scholars, but their theological outlook was that of Lutheran neo-orthodoxy. Troeltsch and
his friends treated them with cool respect, feeling in
their hearts that they were antiques.[11] The only teacher
in Erlangen who made an impression upon them was
the philosopher Gustav Class, a man who, on the basis
of later German Idealism and through dependence upon
Leibniz, endeavored to secure room for religion in the
life of the human intellect. He was sympathetic toward
R. H. Lotze who, just like R. Eucken at a later time, defended, in idealist fashion, the freedom of the spirit
against a positivism determined by the natural sciences.

One of Troeltsch's best friends was Wilhelm Bousset,
who later became one of the most prominent and influential interpreters of the New Testament on the basis of
the history of religion. They were in almost constant
contact with one another for eight years, first as students in Erlangen and in Göttingen, and then as young
instructors in Göttingen. Troeltsch reports [12] that because of the shape of his face and his curly hair, Bousset
was called the "Moor," and Troeltsch invented and
spread the legend that Bousset's grandfather had been a

11. Cf. Ernst Troeltsch, "Die kleine Göttinger Fakultät von 1890,"
Christliche Welt 34 (1920), p. 281.
12. *Ibid.*

moor who, as a member of the band at the ducal court
of Mecklenburg, beat the drums. Bousset in turn told all
sorts of tales about Troeltsch, some of which the latter
had to deny until the end of his life.

One of these is the story of Troeltsch's arrival in
Heidelberg where, not yet thirty years old, he assumed
the chair of systematic theology. According to custom,
he presented himself to all his colleagues in the university by paying them a personal visit. So Troeltsch went
also to see the most distinguished among them, the famous historian of philosophy Kuno Fischer who for
many years was enthroned at Heidelberg as a prince of
scholars and who was notorious for his immense professorial vanity. As Troeltsch entered Fischer's room, he
walked up to him and said in his outgoing, exuberant
way: "My dear colleague, I am so glad finally to make
your personal acquaintance!" Fischer assumed a distant
air and replied: "Address me as 'Your Excellency,' please!"
Then there followed a cool conversation which lasted no
longer than the prescribed seven minutes. Immediately
thereafter, Troeltsch went to the railroad station, assembled all available porters, paid each a handsome tip
and then, having ascertained that the men knew Professor Fischer and where he lived and which route he took
on his way from his house to the university and at what
time of day, he instructed them that, on the following
day, they were to take up posts at different street lamps.
As Fischer passed, each of them was to lift his cap, bow
deeply, and say, "Good morning, Your Excellency!" It is

said that this was actually done and that Professor Fischer acknowledged the salutation as though everything were in proper order.

Troeltsch and Bousset decided to complete their studies in Göttingen. There they came immediately under the influence of Albrecht Ritschl, and theology became for them an exciting branch of learning. They were Ritschl's last pupils. He impressed them by the power of his personality and his utterly unromantic and bourgeois but deeply moral integrity, and they were captivated by the grand conception and design of his theology. They read the New Testament after his fashion and let him inspire them to undertake a close historical study of the Reformation and especially the theology of Luther. They also made it their concern to understand religion independently from naturalism. Troeltsch read H. Lotze who, for many years, had been an influential teacher in Göttingen but who had left there just as Troeltsch arrived. His personalism remained always attractive to Troeltsch. He must have found it reconcilable with Ritschl's teachings, even though Ritschl endeavored to separate religion from philosophy and especially metaphysics. But both Lotze and Ritschl wanted nothing so much as to affirm the supremacy of the human spirit over nature.

Gradually, another influence made itself felt upon Troeltsch's thinking. History became more and more important for him as he began more fully to appreciate the use of the historical method for the proper interpre-

tation of Christianity and its sources. Historical studies
promised to revolutionize theological work. Men like
Wellhausen and Harnack were just then opening new
horizons in studies of the Bible and of the history of
Christian doctrine. In this connection, it proved decisive
for Troeltsch's entire career that he and his friends
came under the influence of Paul de Lagarde who, as an
historian of religion and as a philological expert in lan-
guages, was Ritschl's antipode. He taught them to see
Christianity in the context of the history of religion and
he demanded that strict historical and philological
methods be employed in the interpretation of religious
texts. Troeltsch recognized increasingly Ritschl's one-
sidedness; first of all, his use of the Bible which could
not be justified in terms of an historical interpretation,
and then his modernization of the Reformation and especially of Luther's theology. He also came to suspect
that there was not that continuity between the Reformation and the modern era which was commonly assumed everywhere and which only a few, among them
Lagarde, denied.

He then conceived the plan of describing historically
the process by which Western civilization was formed
in order to assign to the Christian religion its proper
place in this process. In other words, he felt that the
Christian religion should be interpreted in the context
of cultural history. He realized fully how radically such
a program differed from the traditional theological stud-

ies, including ecclesiastical history and the history of doctrine.

When, in 1890, after a brief period of church work as a vicar, he began his career as an academic teacher by becoming a *Privatdozent* in Göttingen, he had the vocational sense that he would revolutionize theology through historical studies. He believed himself supported in this by the enthusiasm of other young men who at the same time acquired the *venia legendi* and who also were engaged primarily in historical investigations. They all referred to themselves as "the little theological faculty of Göttingen," and they were in intimate personal contact with one another and eagerly learned from each other: Wilhelm Bousset; William Wrede; Hermann Gunkel; Albert Eichhorn who were later joined by Johannes Weiss; Wilhelm Heitmüller; and Paul Wernle. Most of them were biblical scholars and as such historians of religion. Troeltsch alone was engaged in systematic theological work, but his chief interest lay in intellectual and cultural history. Troeltsch later wrote about this collaboration as follows: "We had a wonderful time; we were marvelously easy-going and utterly indifferent about the future but the present meant everything to us, for it was full of mutual stimulation and it teamed with new discoveries." [13]

Troeltsch was lucky: already in 1892, he was appointed an associate professor in Bonn and, two years later,

13. *Christliche Welt* 34, p. 282.

he was called to the chair of systematic theology in
Heidelberg. He stayed there until 1915. From 1909 on
he taught also philosophical courses.

IV

He brought into his career two big problems which he
hoped to solve by scholarly investigations.[14] The first,
which was to occupy him during the earlier part of his
lifework, was the problem of the nature of religion in
the context of man's intellectual development. The second, which kept him engaged throughout his life, was
the problem of the historical development of the religious spirit in connection with its imbeddedness in the
universal life process.

Realizing that this program could not possibly be executed because it was much too inclusive, he decided to
concentrate on a part of it for work on which he would
be able to acquire competence in not too long a time.
Without losing sight of the larger question, he set himself the task of analyzing the development of religion in
the context of universal life by concentrating his attention upon Christianity and its connection with Western
cultural history.

He made a beginning with his doctoral dissertation
on *Reason and Revelation in Melanchthon and Johann
Gerhard* (1891). He analyzed first the thought of Me-

14. *Gesammelte Schriften*, IV, 6.

lanchthon in relation to that of Luther and then the teaching of Gerhard, the foremost representative of Lutheran Orthodoxy, in relation to that of Melanchthon. Apart from demonstrating how Orthodoxy had arisen from the Reformation by way of Melanchthon's interpretation of Luther's doctrines by means of Aristotelianism and humanistic rhetorical methods, the result of this study was the conclusion that the thinking of the German Lutherans had remained basically medieval but that, in comparison with medieval scholasticism, they had achieved under the influence of Luther's fresh discovery of the gospel a simplification of Christian theological thought which they combined with certain Stoic ideas, particularly those relating to natural law. These had been part of Christianity for a long time, and, like other ancient materials which Christian thinkers had absorbed, they had been periodically revived. This was happening also in the aftermath of the Reformation.

From here Troeltsch was led to raise the question when and under what circumstances so-called modern civilization had arisen, that is, how it had come about that an autonomous secular culture had come to affirm itself over against a tradition which was bound to the churches and saturated with ecclesiastical dogmas and doctrines. In contrast to the answer commonly given that the Protestant Reformation had laid the foundations of modern civilization, he pointed to the Enlightenment of the eighteenth century. This movement, he argued, had transformed the social-political and eco-

nomic secularization of life, begun in the age of the
Renaissance and in part continued under the auspices of
the Protestant Reformation, into a new educational system with the help of the philosophies of the eighteenth
century, and had pushed the supranatural powers of
church and theology into the background.[15] Specific
studies [16] of the Enlightenment, Deism, the English
Moralists of the eighteenth century, and German Idealism confirmed him in this view. Moreover, he felt that
he had the support of Wilhelm Dilthey with whose historical studies he now became acquainted.

In 1906 Troeltsch published a large work entitled
*Protestant Christianity and Ecclesiasticism in the Mod-
ern Age*,[17] an analytical survey of the development of
Protestantism in its relation to the cultural life. It is a
marvelous piece of work, indeed unique, because no ecclesiastical or secular historian has had knowledge and
courage enough to undertake the same task. It is really
the story of the steady and continual emancipation of
Western civilization from the church or the story of the
gradual secularization of Western culture with special
attention to the relations between Protestantism and
civilization. Troeltsch showed, on the one hand, the

15. *Gesammelte Schriften*, IV, 7.
16. These were published in the form of long articles in *Protes-
tantische Realenzyklopädie*, ed. A. Hauck, 3rd ed. (Leipzig,
1896–1913).
17. Pages 431–755 of Geschichte der Christlichen Religion, *Die
Kultur der Gegenwart*, ed. P. Hinneberg, Vol. I; IV, 1 (Leipzig,
1906; 2nd ed., 1909, 1922).

great difference between the order of Roman Catholicism and the tenets of the Protestant reformers and, on
the other hand, the deep divergence between Old Protestantism and New Protestantism.

At a meeting of German historians in 1906, he presented the same argument in a paper entitled "The Significance of the Reformation for the Rise of the Modern
World." [18] He did not deny that the Protestant reformers had inaugurated a new age in the history of Christianity and he gave full recognition to the fact that they
had destroyed the ecclesiastical unity of European culture, but he reaffirmed his conviction that the forms of
life that were fostered by the reformers and their suc-
cessors, the founders of the Protestant churches, were
more closely related to the Middle Ages than to the
modern world.

At the time, his thesis was generally rejected. One
still adhered to the view which, strangely enough, had
first been expressed by the Enlighteners and then became common among historians, that the Reformation
marked the beginning of modern civilization, because
Martin Luther and his followers had defied, and by
their defiance had undone, the heteronomous authoritarianism of the Roman Church. Today, Troeltsch's interpretation is generally regarded as correct because it
is widely recognized that, in this age, the churches no

18. Curiously enough, this work was published in an English
translation under the title *Protestantism and Progress* (New York,
1912; Boston, 1958).

longer determine the decisions which shape the character of civilization and public life, and that Protestantism
and Roman Catholicism, insofar as they are represented
by ecclesiastical organizations, have more in common
than they share together or singly with the men and
powers that mould modern civilization.

What disturbed Troeltsch especially about traditional
Christianity was the persistence with which representative ecclesiastical bodies and spokesmen adhered to su-
pernaturalism in some form or other. For him Christianity was a religion among religions. He believed that
concerning its nature it must be interpreted epistemo-
logically or psychologically and concerning its historical
forms it must be regarded as subject to an analysis by
methods that are applied to all historical phenomena.

During the first decade of this century, he was a very
active participant of discussions on the philosophy of religion, and he published numerous papers of his own.
In most of them, he pursued arguments that were in
line with what had been begun by Schleiermacher,
though his own philosophical preferences at the time
were formed by his attachment to such neo-Kantians as
Heinrich Rickert and Wilhelm Windelband. But his
deeply passionate interest belonged to historical studies.
All his thinking was filled with the awareness that the
omnipresence in modern cultural life of the sense of history or of the historical consciousness constituted the
most important difference from other ages. He therefore

became preoccupied with questions about the nature of history and of historical knowledge and their importance for the right understanding of religion and its place in human life. He also steeped himself in historical studies as such chiefly because he wanted to know as fully as possible the perils and possibilities of his own age. His reading was very wide. Indeed, his friends always marveled at the rate at which he absorbed book after book.

Thus it is not surprising that he acquired a scholarly reputation chiefly as an historian and as a philosopher of history. Nevertheless, the judgment widely prevailed (and sometimes is expressed even today) that he was the systematic or constructive theologian of the so-called "*religionsgeschichtliche Schule.*" Though he held a chair of systematic theology and therefore regularly lectured on subjects of this discipline, he did not attribute too much importance to it. For he believed that the days of theological summas and systems had passed forever. The individualism which determined the practice of religion everywhere in the Western world and the diversity of religious forms which followed from this made it impossible in his opinion to rally a school of students or a congregation of believers around a system of doctrines. Troeltsch taught courses in systematic theology because he wanted to demonstrate how a person who had acquired the modern world view based on science, history, and philosophy would relate himself to

the heritage of Christian thought. Moreover, he wanted
to prepare his students for the work of spiritual leadership in churches whose members they would have to
treat as modern men and women. In his view, books on
systematic theology, for example, those of Wilhelm
Herrmann, were not works of scholarship, but devo-
tional books.[19]

It is understandable that Troeltsch was no friend of
ecclesiastical governments. They impressed him not
only as too conservative but also as too authoritarian.
He disliked their alliances with political authorities, especially in monarchical Germany and most particularly
in Prussia. He was deeply aroused when these church
bureaucracies interfered with theological scholarship by
trying to influence appointments to academic positions,
or when they staged heresy trials against ministers who
held liberal opinions about liturgy or doctrine, or when
they stirred up bitter public controversies by insisting
on conformity with creeds and confessions of faith. During the first years of Troeltsch's professorial career, Harnack was frequently the center and victim of such trou-
bles, especially in connection with his historical interpretation of the Apostles' Creed (1892) and the publication of his lectures on the "Nature of Christianity"
(1901).

19. See Walther Koehler, *Ernst Troeltsch* (Tübingen, 1941), p.
339.

V

The most representative journal of religious and theological liberalism in Germany was *Die Christliche Welt,* a biweekly founded in 1886 by Martin Rade (1857–1940), one of the earliest pupils of Adolf Harnack and a Ritschlian, like his teacher. He edited it throughout his long life and from 1900 on in Marburg where, in 1903, he became a professor of theology. Around this journal, Rade gathered many loyal readers and supporters and among them also the most influential liberal theological teachers, including also Harnack and Troeltsch.[20] They not only contributed frequently to its columns but they also were active in a loose organization called *Freunde der Christlichen Welt* which met regularly every year for the discussion of common, mainly theological, problems. Troeltsch was intimately connected with this group and eagerly participated in its life, especially in his earlier years. He remained loyal to Rade and *Die Christliche Welt* until the end of his life.

About one of Troeltsch's earliest public appearances in this circle, Walter Koehler (1870–1947), one of his first students who in 1940 published a large interpretative work about his teacher, reports as follows:

20. Johannes Rathje, *Die Welt des freien Protestantismus. Ein Beitrag zur deutsch-evangelischen Geistesgeschichte, dargestellt am Leben und Werk von Martin Rade* (Stuttgart, 1952).

It was in 1896, at a gathering of theologians in Eisenach, that Ernst Troeltsch dramatically burst upon the intellectual scene. One of the most respected of Germany's theological scholars, Julius Kaftan, had just completed a learned, somewhat scholastic lecture on the meaning of the logos-doctrine. With the opening of general discussion, there leaped with youthful élan to the rostrum a young professor who began his statement with the words: "Gentlemen, everything is tottering." Then he went on to outline with large, firm strokes a picture of the situation which was to confirm his judgment. The older scholars were appalled. When their spokesman [Ferdinand Kattenbusch] in turn took the floor, he rejected Troeltsch's line of reasoning as "paltry theology" —at which Troeltsch got up and left, slamming the door behind him.[21]

Troeltsch insisted that everything had evolved and developed—also man and religion. Hence he demanded that Christianity, including Jesus its founder, be interpreted in the context of the history of religion. This was unacceptable to the older Ritschlians, and especially to Kattenbusch, who wrote to Rade early in 1898 that he did not want to be identified with Troeltsch, though he said that personally he liked this "son of nature." [22] But he did not want even to seem to be cooperative with him, for he regarded Troeltsch's position as diametrically different from his own. In an article published in *Die Christliche Welt*, he disclosed this salient point:

21. Cf. W. Koehler, *Troeltsch*, p. 1; also H. Stuart Hughes, *Consciousness and Society: The Reorientation of European Social Thought, 1890–1930* (New York, 1958), pp. 229f.
22. Cf. Rathje, *Die Welt des freien Protestantismus*, p. 94. Letter to Rade (17 January 1898): *"ich mag den Naturburschen leiden."*

"We older Ritschlians," he wrote, "see in Christianity a
factor at work that has entered history from without." [23] In agreement with Ritschl himself, he believed
this factor, namely, the revelation in Jesus, to be supernatural or at least superhistorical. Troeltsch replied to
this by saying that the Ritschlians, in order to maintain
the autonomy and independence of the Christian religion and theology, had the tendency to push aside difficulties that arose from history just as they were avoiding coming to terms theologically with the methods and
findings of the natural sciences.[24] Instead he felt that it
was necessary to acknowledge in principle the historiza-
tion of theology. Hence the historical method would
have to replace the dogmatic method in theology, that
is, the procedure which permitted the interpretation of
religious data, particularly those pertaining to Christianity, to be dictated by purely dogmatic ideas or
teachings. Thus Troeltsch envisaged a nondogmatic or
undogmatic Christianity. "Religion as such can get
along without dogmatics," he observed.[25]

In 1902 he drew the consequences from this position
by publishing a long essay on "The Absoluteness of
Christianity and the History of Religions." He rejected
all arguments for the absoluteness of Christianity that
were based either on the affirmation of external or inter-
nal miracles, as Orthodox and Pietist theologians, and
even the Ritschlians, were doing or on the Hegelian as-

23. *Ibid.*, p. 106; *C.W.* 3 (98) nos. 3 and 4.
24. Cf. *Ibid.*, p. 106; *C.W.* 3 (98) nos. 27–28.
25. Cf. *Ibid.*, p. 109.

sertion that the development of religion had reached its climax in Christianity, the embodiment of religion itself. Instead he argued that all high religions "naively" advance claims for absoluteness which cannot effectively be refuted. He was prepared to ascribe a certain superiority to Christianity because he believed that because of its ethics it exercised a universal appeal upon all men, an appeal for which he saw no parallel in any other faith. He realized that if this view were correct, foreign missions as carried out traditionally could no longer be defended, and he did not hesitate to draw this conclusion, especially in the light of the fact which he regarded as insurmountable, namely, that all high religions have entered, in the course of their development, into a union with historical cultures which no effort to displace the religious faith with the intent to substitute for it another one can effectively or justifiably dissolve.

Many problems arose for Troeltsch from this position. The foremost ones were the following: (1) the philosophical question: how can the truth of religion be ascertained? and (2) the historical question: how is the correlation between religion and culture to be explained?

Troeltsch gave full attention to both, always in the context of an animated discussion with other thinkers and researchers. Though he continued to be active and productive as a philosopher of religion, his major interest was now more and more directed to the problems of the theology of culture.

The richness and diversity of the historical world fascinated him. With ever greater force the question of the nature and direction of modern Western civilization impressed itself upon his mind. He became involved in political action (for several years, he represented the University of Heidelberg in the upper house of parliament in the Grand Duchy of Baden) and in discussions of social policy. All this called forth the question of how he could find a grounding for truth and value in the flow of all things human.[26] In his thinking on the philosophy of history, he had let his outlook be determined chiefly by Hegel and Dilthey. Now they no longer satisfied him fully. The problems of intellectual history seemed to him much more complicated than they made them appear, especially in view of the hard practical realities in which the intellectual and spiritual concerns of men are imbedded. He plunged into sociological studies and learned a new way of seeing things.[27] At the same time, he came under the spell of the overwhelmingly powerful person of Max Weber.

VI

Thus began a highly fruitful association of two scholars, each of whom was occasionally described by others as a genius. Neither of them, though an expert in his own

26. Cf. Hughes, *Consciousness and Society*, p. 231.
27. Cf. *Gesammelte Schriften*, IV, 11.

field, was a mere specialist. The interests of both ranged far over the realm of human civilization, and both were passionate contemporaries of their own era.

When they became acquainted with one another, Max Weber, who had started out as a legal scholar and had then taken up the teaching of economics and political science, had turned to sociological investigations. He was already at work on his famous essay on "Protestant Ethics and the Spirit of Capitalism" and on the manifold problems of economic ethics which he was to analyze and discuss in the large works he later published. He was "a man of enormous intellectual power and versatility who barely held together by force of an iron resolve the desperate contradictions that threatened his sanity." [28] Troeltsch wrote later: "For years I experienced in daily contact with him the infinitely stimulating power of this man, and I am aware of owing him a great part of my knowledge and ability." [29]

The two men were of different temperaments. Weber was a man of stubborn persistency who could grow ferocious when he felt it necessary to oppose political actions he thought stupid or irresponsible (he despised William II!) or when he believed his personal honor to be attacked. Troeltsch was much more conciliatory, ever prepared to settle differences with others and to adjust himself to their weaknesses. In referring to this

28. Hughes, *Consciousness and Society*, p. 19.
29. Troeltsch, *Deutscher Geist und Westeuropa*, ed. H. Baron (Tübingen, 1925), p. 249.

friendship in the biography of her husband, Marianne
Weber characterizes Troeltsch in the following way:
"Freedom and comprehensiveness of mind; an outgoing
vivaciousness; a plastic and concrete way of thinking;
broad humor and an immediate personal warmth made
him a companion with whom scholarly and personal relations became enjoyable and fruitful." [30]

In 1905 Professor and Mrs. Weber and Troeltsch
made a trip to the United States. They had been invited
to address the "Scientific World Congress" which Professor Hugo Münsterberg had organized in connection
with the World's Fair in St. Louis.[31] Troeltsch delivered a lecture on "Psychology and Epistemology in the
Science of Religion." Together and separately, they
traveled through the eastern and southern states. Troeltsch's humor and pealing laughter enlivened the party,
and Weber's curiosity and power of close and discrimi-
nating observation gave the journey the character of a
scientific exploration. Weber gathered material for his
theory concerning the interrelations between Puritan asceticism and the capitalistic mentality.[32] They must
have talked and debated about these issues as they
moved about in this country.

In support of this, I can tell the following amusing

30. Marianne Weber, *Max Weber: Ein Lebensbild* (Tübingen,
1926), p. 240.
31. Harnack also came to the United States on this occasion.
32. See the chapter on "The Asceticism of the Puritan Sects in
Calvinist Ethics," *The Spirit of Capitalism and the Ethics of
Protestantism* (New York, 1930), pp. 95–154.

story: Many years ago, I became acquainted with a
minister named Hans Haupt. He was the son of a theological professor in the University of Halle in Germany
and he was married to the daughter of a professor of
economics in the same institution. He came to this
country around 1900 and settled in Towanda, New
York, where he became the minister of a German-Evan-
gelical Church. Because of his family connections he
was often visited and consulted by German academic
persons who desired information about American religious and ecclesiastical developments. He also published occasional articles about the United States in
German journals. Troeltsch and Weber informed him of
their impending voyage and of their intention to visit
him. Telling him about their research project, they
asked him to collect as much material as possible about
American denominations and their moral teachings and
attitudes, especially in relation to economic practices.
Haupt immediately went to work and, with considerable difficulty, laid hold of the desired information.
When his distinguished visitors arrived, they spent several days with him. In between an inspection of the
town of Towanda and visits to nearby Niagara Falls,
they talked and argued all the time. But they hardly
asked for Haupt's opinion and failed to inspect the material he had gathered, but they took it with them.
Haupt had the impression that the professors knew all
that could be known without having to weigh empirical
evidence. In fairness to them, one must say that, though

Haupt may have had reasons for complaint about their behavior, they (and particularly Max Weber) made extensive use of factual data and statistics when they explicated their thesis about the nature of Calvinist economic ethics.

The friendship between Weber and Troeltsch deepened during the following years. In the fall of 1909, they moved into a big old house situated on the river Neckar, Weber taking the lower and Troeltsch the upper floor. The closest relationship prevailed between them. They enjoyed and relaxed in the natural beauty of Old Heidelberg, and their house became the intellectual center of the academic community. But all this came to an unhappy end. It is tragic that the bonds of this friendship were broken because of weakness.

When World War I broke out, several of the hospitals and clinics of Heidelberg were transformed into military hospitals.[33] Weber, who was a reserve officer, was put in charge of them. In this capacity, he permitted a few German civilians (who had family ties with Frenchmen) to visit French prisoners of war who were placed in these hospitals. It so happened that Troeltsch had accepted the assignment to serve as the civilian administrator of one of these military hospitals. When he learned that public opinion was becoming aroused because of the visits that were being paid to the French and that the visitors were being accused of treason, he

33. On the following, see Eduard Baumgarten, *Max Weber: Werk und Person* (Tübingen, 1964), p. 624.

decided to permit the visits only if the visitors were accompanied by a military person. When Weber was informed of this, he became greatly agitated and accused his friend of cowardice and lack of courage in view of the invalid and inhumane public rumors. To be sure, he apologized afterwards for his vehemence but at the same time expected Troeltsch to see the error of his ways. But no excuses came forth from him and so the break remained. Only five years later, their wives succeeded in bringing about a reconciliation of sorts.[34] By that time, Troeltsch was in Berlin and Weber in Munich. Close association was no longer possible anyway.

In 1917 Troeltsch wrote to a friend about this as follows:

In the course of the war, Max Weber has assumed such radical attitudes and he views the whole situation so pessimistically and with so much hostility that he has become totally isolated; he has fallen out with most people, including me. Older differences concerning politics and general principles came to the fore in him, and he broke off relations with me in the most violent fashion for no special reason. In the last resort, his life is a continuous duel with everything that he regards as corruptive, and in particular with the person of the Emperor whom he holds responsible for practically everything. It is impossible to argue with him. You can imagine that I am sorry about this. I certainly did not want this to happen.[35]

What was in the background of this unfortunate episode was, of course, the war situation. It forced men

34. Weber, *Lebensbild,* p. 532.
35. To Paul Honigsheim. Cf. Baumgarten, *Max Weber,* p. 489.

like Troeltsch and Weber to make political judgments that were very difficult not only objectively but also subjectively. H. Stuart Hughes is quite correct when he writes: "Both of them, Weber the earliest and most decisively . . . Troeltsch not until the war years—were to cross the invisible barricade that separated the opponents from the supporters of the régime. And they did it with the deepest sorrow, driven against their will by the irresponsible behavior of the Emperor, the calamitous mistakes in foreign policy, the unyielding resistance to the democratization of the constitution of Prussia and of the Reich. . . . With each year of the postponed reform, they felt the chances growing dimmer of saving their country from a major catastrophe." [36]

Undoubtedly, Troeltsch became politically active, especially in relation to foreign affairs, under the influence of Weber, and he remained so until the end of his life. But the major lesson which he learned from him at the beginning of their association and which he developed fully as an interpreter of Christian history was that the Christian faith like any other high religion is and has been a powerful formative factor in social relations. He learned not only that there exists an interconnection between Protestantism and modern economic attitudes and practices but also that the origin, development, and the modern containment of Christianity have been sociologically conditioned. Moreover, he came to see, again under the impact of Weber's views, that the Marxist interpretation of history, and particularly the doctrine of

36. Hughes, *Consciousness and Society*, p. 49.

economic substructures and ideological superstructures, was largely true. He wrote later that all this took hold of him "with greatest force." [37]

There existed then no historical or systematic studies on the interconnection between Christianity and society. When Troeltsch was asked to review what he thought was a "miserable" book by M. von Nathusius on *The Social Responsibility of the Evangelical Church,* he became forcefully aware of his own as well as the general ignorance about the social aspects of religion. Without taking time first to outline carefully a program of study, he went to work, and instead of a book review he wrote a volume comprising nearly a thousand pages entitled *The Social Teachings of the Christian Churches and Denominations.*[38] "This was," to use his own words, "a history of the ecclesiastical culture of Christianity, a full parallel to Harnack's *History of Dogma,* in which all religious, dogmatic, and theological factors were seen as the basis of social-ethical effects or as the reflection or retroaction of social conditions."

He concentrated his attention upon the social teachings of the Christian groups in order to illuminate the relation between the impetus for action that issued from the faith of Christians throughout the generations and the actual state of things prevailing at different times

37. *Gesammelte Schriften,* IV, 11.
38. First published in the form of long articles between 1908 and 1910, then as Vol. I of Troeltsch's *Gesammelte Schriften* in 1912. In 1931, an English translation (by Olive Wyon) appeared.

and places. The result was that he gave a much more complex and dynamic picture of the development of Christianity than that which is offered by church historians who see this development primarily in relation to its environmental background or by historians of doctrine who tend to deal only with Christian intellectual history. Surveying Christian social history from the beginning to the eighteenth century, focusing his attention mainly upon Roman Catholicism and Protestantism, and omitting a full treatment either of Eastern Orthodoxy or of Anglicanism, he showed how what he called the eschatological ethical utopianism of the early Christians emitted from itself an impetus that broke into the orders of ancient society and changed them, being at the same time affected by them—like a giant spring that as it rises breaks the rock formation in which it originates and then, becoming a torrent and river, makes its way to the sea being channeled by the formation of the earth through which it passes, but carrying with it masses of rock and soil which it absorbs.

He clarified many things of which I mention here only a few: (1) He showed that Christian moral and social doctrines have never been expressions of a pure religious spirit or of an absolute ethic but have always been compromises,[39] that is, results of a mediating syn-

39. Cf. John R. Hanson, "Ernst Troeltsch's Concept of Compromise," *Lutheran Quarterly*, XVIII (1966), pp. 351–361. Also James L. Adams, "Ernst Troeltsch as Analyst of Religion," in *Journal for the Scientific Study of Religion*, I (1961), p. 105.

thesis by which Christian individuals and groups have
come to terms with their environments, even with elements alien to their spirit. Troeltsch used this concept
of compromise throughout his career. In one of his last
pieces of writing, he said: "The fact remains that all in-
transigeance breaks down in practice and can only end
in disaster. The history of Christianity itself is most in-
structive in this connection. It is, in the long run, a tremendous, continuous compromise between the utopian
demands of the Kingdom of God and the permanent
conditions of the actual human life. It was indeed a
sound instinct which led its founders to look for a
speedy dissolution of the present world order."

(2) He demonstrated the importance of this observation chiefly by pointing to the place which since ancient
times was given in Christian social affairs to natural law
as defined by the Stoics and the Aristotelians. This
made possible, in medieval Catholicism, the remarkable
synthesis between nature and grace, Aristotelianism and
biblicism, world and church, indeed shaped the ethics
of all Western Christianity, including that of the major
Protestant churches.

(3) In describing the major forms of Christian social
organization, Troeltsch distinguished between churches
and sects. In doing so, he followed Weber who had used
this distinction in his studies of Calvinism. For him the
terms "church" and "sect" referred to sociological models or ideal types as they must be used in all sociological
or historical analyses for purposes of clarification and

classification.[40] Actual social orders or organizations do
not necessarily represent what these models as genetic
concepts symbolize. Perhaps Troeltsch used them too
rigidly or mechanically [41] as if the basic definition of
"church" and "sect" could be regarded as the description
of empirical reality. For this he has been much criticized.
But it is undeniable that as he analyzed the relevance of
these concepts to the historical development of Christian social groups and their orders and works, he made
possible a clear and suggestive understanding of the sociological processes that have moulded the Christian encounter with the world. The suggestiveness of his analysis is expressed in the definition of the basic concepts
which he offers in the "conclusion" of *The Social Teachings:*

The *Church* is the holy institution and the institution of
grace, endowed with the effect and result of the work of
redemption. It can absorb the masses and adapt itself to
the world, since, up to a certain point, it can neglect sub-
jective holiness in exchange for the objective treasures of
grace and redemption. The *Sect* is the free association of
Christians who are stronger and more conscious of their
faith. They join together as the truly reborn, separate themselves from the world, remain limited to a small circle,
emphasize the law instead of grace, and in their ranks set
up love as the Christian order of life with greater or lesser

40. Cf. Benjamin A. Reist, *Toward a Theology of Involvement:
The Thought of Ernst Troeltsch* (Philadelphia, 1966), pp.
106 ff.
41. Cf. Hughes, *Consciousness and Society,* p. 235.

radicalism. All of this is regarded as the preparation for
and the expectation of the coming Kingdom of God. *Mysti-
cism* is the intensification and the subjectivization of the
thoughts and ideas that have become solidified in cult and
doctrine so that they are a purely personal and inner possession of the heart. Under its auspices only fluid and completely personally limited groups can assemble. What remains
in them of cult, dogma, and connection with history tends to
become so fluid that it disappears.[42]

Troeltsch laid special emphasis upon Roman Catholicism and Calvinism. They appeared to him as the most
effective social orders in Christendom. "The Roman
Catholic or Papal church type" he wrote,[43] "is undoubtedly the most unified and most effective church type,
practically as well as logically most completely formed.
The Calvinist church type closely approached the sect-
type, in the course of its history, and in connection with
legal, political, social, and economic developments incorporated its pharisaic-democratic characteristics in
huge mass-movements." [44]

Troeltsch said once: "I have carried my *Social Teachings* only to the eighteenth century and this for a good
reason. From that time on, European Civilization can no
longer be called Christian. (*Die offizielle Christlichkeit*

42. *Gesammelte Schriften,* I, 967. Cf. Reist, *Toward a Theology
of Involvement,* p. 116.
43. *In Zeitschrift für Theologie und Kirche* (Tübingen, 1920), p.
119.
44. Here Troeltsch probably had in mind the rise of American
denominationalism on the Frontier, i.e., the Methodists and Bap-
tists and evangelical movements.

Europas ist mit ihm zu Ende.)" [45] He was deeply convinced that beginning with the period of the Enlightenment, and particularly since the rise of High Capitalism
and the formation of the big political powers, Western
civilization has become emancipated from the shaping
and unifying influence of the old Christian institutions,
with the result that it is being exposed more and more
to secularization and secularism.

He became increasingly involved in the effort to understand "modern civilization" or "the modern era of
Western civilization" and to achieve the vision of a cultural synthesis, as he called it, in which the values of
the Christian cultural heritage would be preserved and
incorporated in the common life. So he turned more and
more to studies on ethics and the philosophy of history.

To some extent, he had outgrown the faculty of theology. When he received a call to the University of Berlin in order to teach philosophy with special attention to
the philosophy of history and the philosophy of religion,
he accepted. [46]

VII

It was the spring of 1915 and World War I was still in
its first undecisive stages. Heidelberg seemed to him a

45. Cf. Dietrich, *Biographisches Jahrbuch* (1923), p. 355.
46. Cf. the article by Ulrich Pretzel, "E. Troeltsch's Berufung an
die Berliner Universität," in *Studium Berolinense* (Berlin, 1960),
pp. 507–514.

little provincial; some of his closest friends (for example, the jurist George Jellinek) had died; he was estranged from Max Weber; his relations with the circle of friends of *Die Christliche Welt* were no longer as warm as they had been earlier. He also felt that the philosophy of religion rather than systematic theology was his field of specialization. It is not true as it is frequently stated that he forsook the theological faculty because he believed that his own theological work had ended in failure. In the autobiographical sketch of his literary production, he says specifically: "I have at all times fulfilled the practical educational tasks assigned to the theological faculty with warmest respect for the great subject and with personal love for my students. I considered dogmatics as a practical concern in which lack of clarity and the insecurity of human knowledge play an essentially important role but which nevertheless permits the main value of practical religion to be communicated to the hearts of the students as a burning and propulsive power." [47] And in another context of the same paper he wrote: "If I stay healthy and alive, I should like to return to the study of religion in order to complete my philosophy of religion. This is my first love." [48]

At the beginning of this essay, I described Troeltsch's great influence and success as a teacher and lecturer in Berlin. It is not necessary to elaborate this theme fur-

47. *Gesammelte Schriften*, IV, 12.
48. *Ibid.*, p. 15.

ther. But what I must stress is that in Berlin he rapidly assumed the stature of a great public figure. During the period when the form and constitution of the new German Republic took shape, his name was sometimes mentioned as that of a possible and worthy candidate for the post of president.

He had occasion to observe closely the setting, complexity, and agony in which political decisions are made when he became intimately acquainted with the Chancellor Bethmann von Hollweg, that rather tragic figure who, despite his faults and failures, deserves high human respect. He also assumed responsibility in the moulding of public opinion as a public speaker and as an author of articles. He joined the still small circles of professors and members of the upper middle classes who opposed the war aims of the militarists and annexationists in the conservative parties. He identified himself with men like Harnack, Hans Delbrück, and Friedrich Meinecke,[49] who advocated inner political and social reforms and who warned their countrymen of the dangers of an excessive nationalism. When the war was lost, he joined those who undertook the tasks of cultural and political reconstruction. "In these bitter years of national discouragement and civil conflict," says H. Stuart Hughes, who is inclined to be rather critical of Troeltsch's philosophical thought,

49. In his autobiography, F. Meinecke describes in detail his and his friends' involvement in these struggles. He pays special attention to E. Troeltsch. See *Erlebtes, 1862–1891* (Stuttgart, 1964), pp. 258 ff. and 266 ff.

Troeltsch at last found his authentic voice. The monthly articles he contributed to the review *Der Kunstwart* under the signature *Spektator*[50] rank as the most judicious and at the same time the most moving commentary on the new Republic's struggle for existence. Where in his theological and philosophical writings Troeltsch had been dense, wordy, and confused, in this new journalistic and polemical vein, he went directly to the point . . . The "Spectator Letters" belong in that rare category of occasional pieces that have won immortality. The frightful demagoguery and provocation from the right, which Troeltsch very clearly recognized as the symptoms of a new barbarism that might arise in the future, made, he felt, the task of a responsible German government almost impossible. Only if leading citizens should acquiesce in democracy . . . "with inner warmth" would it be possible to build the future. And then alone would it be possible to salvage and restore those broader values of humanism and rationality that Troeltsch . . . had most at heart.[51]

VIII

In 1922 there appeared what was to be Troeltsch's last publication, a large volume entitled *Der Historismus und seine Probleme*.[52] It contained a series of learned articles in which the work of modern historians and philosophers of history was reviewed in considerable detail

50. After Troeltsch's death Meinecke collected and published these articles in one volume: *Spektatorbriefe* (München, 1924).
51. Hughes, *Consciousness and Society,* p. 379.
52. *Gesammelte Schriften,* III.

with special attention to the concepts of historical individuality, historical norms, and historical development. The book differs from most works on the nature and meaning of history because its pages are filled with a profound passion. On the one hand, there is the affirmation which is reiterated again and again that in the modern world all human life has become historicized, that is, that all human decisions, undertakings, and conditions are determined by historical factors so that everything human appears to be set in changing historical relations. On the other hand, there is expressed a deep concern about the possibility that this relativism may lead to an anarchy of values and to scepticism and nihilism.[53] Hence he makes a great effort to show how "history can be overcome by history," [54] that is, how by live historical decisions one can avoid becoming entangled in historicism. These live historical decisions which must be made by individuals as well as by groups relate to the cultural heritage insofar as it is apprehended in any given present. It must be understood, evaluated, and judged. Thus it becomes transformed, that is, reduced or enlarged. That in it which is judged to be

53. F. Meinecke recalled ("E. Troeltsch und das Problem des Historismus," in *Werke*, IV: *Zur Theorie und Philosophie der Geschichte* [Stuttgart, 1959], p. 369) that Troeltsch once referred "with some horror to the remark of the master of the art of historical empathy, Dilthey, when in the evening of his life he spoke of the 'anarchy of convictions' (*die Anarchie der Uberzeugungen*); (cf. W. Dilthey, *Gesammelte Schriften*, V, 9) which would in the end be the consequence of modern historical thought."
54. *Gesammelte Schriften*, III, 772.

valid only for the past out of which it has come is rele-
gated to the past or, as Schleiermacher said in a mem-
orable passage of his *Glaubenslehre*,[55] entrusted to history for safekeeping. And that in it which is recognized
as of value for the present is incorporated in present action by way of a renaissance or a reformation. These
historical assessments and actions undertaken in the
present thus appropriate a legacy of past generations for
the use of generations to come. This responsibility is
carried out everywhere in human society in great cultural enterprises undertaken on vast public platforms as
well as in the execution of small programs which remain
confined to privacy. The historical sense which is expressed in this is often unconscious, but from time to
time, and according to the requirement of the circumstances in which it is brought into play, it needs to be
refined and sharpened by historical scholarship and the
assistance of historical experts.

In this sense, the interest in history was for Troeltsch
something eminently practical. "The merely contemplative view of history is something unnatural and sense-
less," he wrote.

It leads to a bad historism insofar as in it there is displayed
an unlimited relativism, a playful occupation with the historical materials, and a paralysis of the will to live one's own
life. The personal interest of the spectator then turns into
the enjoyment of the play of the phenomena and the diver-

55. F. Schleiermacher, *The Christian Faith*, trans. H. R. Mackin-
tosh and J. S. Stewart (Edinburgh, 1928), p. 475.

sity of happenings; into the readiness of comprehending and excusing everything; into a mere interest in knowledge or even into a scepticism that may issue in sophisticated irony or, in the case of people of hard temperaments, in sarcasm, or, in the case of the kindhearted, in humor.[56]

For him a practical historicism or an "activist philosophy of history"[57] consisted of the proposition of a cultural synthesis or program based on an historical analysis or interpretation of Europeanism or Western civilization. He intended to outline this synthesis in a second volume devoted to the theme of historicism. But he died before he could write it. It would have been a summary of the results of his entire work. In lectures which he intended to deliver in England in March of 1923, he offered a moving outline of this. Fortunately, he had prepared these lectures far in advance. And so they could be published. The English translation was given the rather innocuous title of *Christian Thought: Its History and Application*.[58] The German version was more

56. *Gesammelte Schriften*, III, 61.
57. This is his own phrase: *Gesammelte Schriften*, III, 13.
58. The editor and chief translator of this volume was Baron Friedrich von Hügel. It was he on whose initiative Troeltsch had been invited to lecture in England. Indeed, von Hügel himself had made the engagements for Troeltsch's prospective visits to Oxford, London, and Edinburgh in March 1923. As he himself writes in his introduction and in an appreciative, yet not uncritical essay on Troeltsch which is included in the first volume of his *Essays and Addresses on the Philosophy of Religion* (London, 1921), he had concerned himself with Troeltsch's published writings since 1896. He was attracted to Troeltsch because he believed that Troeltsch was interested in the same problems that engaged his own attention. Moreover, he was persuaded that he

adequately if somewhat presumptuously entitled *Die
Überwindung des Historismus* (*The Triumph over
Historicism*). Troeltsch really did not believe that his-

could learn much from Troeltsch's vast scholarship. It is interesting to hear from him that he, the Roman Catholic layman, believed to have received from Troeltsch a true understanding of
Thomas Aquinas (he referred, in this connection, to the *Social
Teachings*). In April of 1901 he spent a week with Troeltsch in
Heidelberg. This was the only time when the two met each other
personally. They remained in touch with one another by correspondence. World War I interrupted the correspondence but it
was resumed, on von Hügel's initiative, in 1920.

After Troeltsch's death, von Hügel published part of the correspondence in *Die Christliche Welt* (1923; pp. 312ff.). We can
obtain from these letters some information about Troeltsch's pri-
vate life. Thus we learn, for example, that Troeltsch got married
in 1901 and that his marriage, to his own great sorrow, remained
childless until 1913 when (in July) a son was born to him. This
event caused Troeltsch (as others of his friends have also written)
to be overjoyed.

In the first letter which Troeltsch sent to von Hügel after World
War I, he wrote: "All of us are grieving over the death of loved
ones. When war broke out, my mother suffered a stroke and she
died soon after. After her death, my father had a complete break-
down; he remained alive for two more years without knowing that
we were at war. My sister lost her only son; he was killed after
only fourteen days of war-service. The health of my brother-in-law
was so much upset by this that he died a year later." (p. 312) It
is no wonder that in another letter, written somewhat later,
Troeltsch was moved to write to his friend: "That man must be
considered happy whom death has freed from the madness of this
world! Whoever must stay on this earth a while longer, must
strain the love for his fellow men not a little in order to endure
them. But, fortunately, the love for men is in the last resort and
properly speaking, not love for men but love for God which loves
that in man which is divine and not the poor confused creature as
such" (p. 314).

One can understand that von Hügel was led to remark that

toricism in the good and true sense of the term could be overcome. He was persuaded that it could be made the platform for responsible and constructive action.

Thus he said at the conclusion of his lecture on "Mankind's Common Spirit":

The task of the damming and controlling of the stream of historical life is . . . on all sides complicated. It involves a combination of the various fundamental tendencies of the ethical consciousness and the only evidence which can ever be deduced for the decisive combinations is but a conviction of faith based on conscience and conditioned by individuality. The solution thus gained . . . can only be spread from individual centers, and made into a spirit of self-communication and love which will as far as possible spread itself over the widest circles, but will always be at war with other forms of belief . . .

With these complex forces it is possible to dam and control the stream of life. But every such control is always . . . a struggle; it is ever changing; it develops ethical public spirit along various lines, and only exceptionally and in a narrower circle is it of centrally binding force. Inasmuch as no unified church any longer exercises this binding force, the task has devolved upon a number of churches and also, along with them, upon personal associations and leagues which are a substitute for the churches, and will themselves have to strive to become a kind of church.

The task of damming and controlling is therefore essen-

Troeltsch lacked lightheartedness and a sense of humor. But this characterization is undoubtedly not correct. What Heinrich Hofmann says (*Theologische Blätter* [1923], p. 77) is much more appropriate: "Despite a gaiety which occasionally even overflowed, he was deeply sensitive of the dark sides of existence, its enigmatic character, and the pain and guilt with which it is filled."

tially incapable of completion and essentially unending; and yet it is always soluble and practicable in each new case. A radical and absolute solution does not exist ، . . History within itself cannot be transcended . . . In history itself there are only relative victories.[59]

In expressing his deepest conviction in this manner, Troeltsch did not speak as a sceptic, as some have surmised, or as one who because of his relativism was uncertain of the truth. He felt that he was testifying to the truth.

A truth which, in the first instance, is *a truth for us* does not cease, because of this, to be very truth and life. What we learn daily through our love for our fellow men, namely, that they are independent beings with standards of their own, we ought also to be able to learn through our love for mankind as a whole—that here too there exist autonomous civilizations with standards of their own . . . In our earthly experience the Divine Life is not One but Many. But to apprehend the One in the Many constitutes the special character of love.[60]

What lies behind these sentences represents Troeltsch's religious faith. In 1907 he expressed it in these words: "Truth is always polymorph, never monomorph; it manifests itself in different forms and kinds, not in different degrees." [61] All these many finite forms of truth, he believed, are part of the one infinite divine life and are suspended in it. "All historical religions," he wrote at the end of his lecture of 1923 on "Christianity

59. *Christian Thought* (New York, 1923 and 1957), p. 144.
60. *Ibid.*, p. 23.
61. Cf. Koehler, *Ernst Troeltsch*, p. 1.

among the World Religions," "are tending in the same
direction, and . . . seem impelled by an inner force to
strive upward towards some unknown final height
where alone the ultimate unity and the final validity can
lie. And, as all religion has thus a common goal in the
Unknown, the Future, perchance in the Beyond, so too
it has a common ground in the Divine Spirit ever pressing the finite mind onward towards further light and
fuller consciousness, a Spirit which indwells the finite
Spirit and whose ultimate union with it is the purpose
of the whole many-sided process." [62]

62. *Christian Thought*, p. 61. At the end of his life, Troeltsch was
clearly filled with a certain pessimism. He was not sure whether
Western civilization could still bring forth creative, reconstructive
forces. His mind was filled with dark forebodings: He feared the
outbreak of a new world conflict, and the behavior of certain radical nationalist groups in Germany led him to conclude that possibly Germany might fall victim to a new barbarism (cf. his *Spektatorbriefe*). He was greatly impressed by Oswald Spengler's *De-
cline of the West*.

In her novel already quoted, Gertrud von le Fort describes
Troeltsch's dark outlook in the following moving passages: "He
said that the professors had no keys with which to open the mystical door of metaphysics. Nobody can unlock this door, he said, all
one can do is to explode it, so to speak. We cannot assure ourselves of the ultimate mysteries except by a bold leap into their
depth. This leap is an enormous daring; it is an entirely personal
decision, but we can act on it despite the dangers and the appar-
ent uncertainty that are involved in it, because it is no blind accident that we entertain such and such ideas about the ultimate
mysteries, for these ideas are effected in us by the divine life itself. (He did not say "effected by God" but "by the divine life").
In our own civilization all essential ideas of the ultimate mysteries
are determined and maintained by Christianity" (*Der Kranz der
Engel*, p. 210).

A little later, there follows this passage: "I expressed gratitude

IX

On 13 January 1923 he fell ill with heart trouble and on
1 February he died. A friend of his, the wife of a former
Heidelberg professor, who visited him in the last days
of his life, writes about him as follows:

Now we have lost also Troeltsch, who was always so full of
vitality . . . It seems that, for some time, his heart gave him
quiet warnings, but he was not wont to save himself. He
had never been ill. He stated sometime ago that he could not
be stingy with his strength and that he would rather have a
short life filled to the brim. There was an unceasing heighten-
ing of his life in the last months. Foreign institutions recognized and honored him in many ways, then came his election
as dean [of the philosophical faculty in Berlin], then his appointment to full membership in the Academy of Sciences [63]

for his lectures and the inward strengthening I had derived from
them.
    He replied: 'Oh, all I have been able to do for you is that I
showed you the sunset of Christianity. When the sun has set, it
still glows for a long time.'
    'Does not the sunset promise a new dawn?' I quickly asked. 'You
too believe, don't you, that the sun will rise again?'
    'I do not know,' he said, honestly. 'No, I really do not know
that; but then, we do not need to know everything. What I do
know is that it is possible to stay alive with a great sunset.'
    'But can the sunset last long?' I asked."
63. It was mainly on the initiative of Harnack that Troeltsch
was elected a full member of the Berlin Academy. In earlier elec-
tions he had been turned down, in all probability because of his
political views. Cf. F. Meinecke, *Erlebtes,* p. 282.

—in his personal and public life he was reaping a rich, fruitful harvest. Then suddenly, with a tremendous pain, sickness befell him—an embolism of the lung caused by the heart itself.[64]

Adolf von Harnack delivered the funeral oration and in giving moving utterance to his own personal loss of one who had been his friend, he characterized Troeltsch beautifully. He called him the representative German philosopher of his own era. He expressed his astonishment at Troeltsch's enormous power of absorption and at his incredible industry. "It is unbelievable," he said, "how much he read day after day," always taking in knowledge in order to produce knowledge. He also remarked on Troeltsch's wonderful power of combination and on the fact that, while he read, he readily thought of something that was better, more important, and more comprehensive. He praised Troeltsch's thoughtfulness and his tolerant spirit. But, he said, Troeltsch despised the distortions of the rationalists and the extravagance of the systematicians. Then he went on to describe Troeltsch's person and character:

How he spoke when he lectured was very peculiar and, at the same time, fascinating. He did not aim at giving sharp and precise formulations but with ever fresh efforts and with an overflowing eloquence which was always abundantly at his command, he tossed an observation or an idea to and fro, attacking it from all sides and placing it in ever different relations, until it seemed to be purified and

64. The letter is printed in Marianne Weber's memoirs, *Lebenserinnerungen* (Bremen, 1948), p. 351.

clear. His mind acted like a powerful centrifugal machine or like a rotating drum which shakes the object and pushes it around until it is cleansed from all foreign elements and until it lights up its own distinctiveness.

He was a splendid man and a good fellow in the best sense of this word. There was in him an elemental power and an abundance of light and life. He was at all times upright and sincere, honest and frank. There was nothing about him that was contrived or petty. But in this powerful person of elemental naturalness there lived a quiet, noble, and pure soul and this was what was best and deepest about him. At the core of his disposition, there was a tenderness and a chaste love.

Few creative men who have become famous have been praised by their peers as Troeltsch was by Harnack!

Appendix

Harnack's Estimate of Troeltsch and Troeltsch's Estimate of Harnack

Note: A. von Harnack published his oration on Troeltsch in a volume of essays entitled *Erforschtes und Erlebtes* (Giessen, 1923), pp. 360–367.

Ernst Troeltsch's essay on Harnack first appeared in *Festgabe für Adolf von Harnack,* ed. Karl Holl (Tübingen, 1921), pp. 282–291.

I

Adolf von Harnack and Ferdinand Christian von Baur 1921

A contribution to a *Festschrift* dedicated to Harnack
on the occasion of his 7oth birthday

by Ernst Troeltsch

After F. C. von Baur, Adolf von Harnack is the first who
has again made church history the sum and substance
of theology and has thereby given it a central position
in those intellectual sciences which deal historically
with the character and origin of our civilization. To
what extent this similarity with Baur depends upon a
broad and deep native talent, upon a full and accurate
knowledge, and upon persistent and comprehensive labor, I cannot explain here inasmuch as I wish to honor
the celebrated master not by general praise but by a
modest description of the impact of his accomplish-
ments upon the younger generation.

It is the identity of accomplishment and influence
which causes me to point out this parallel. For I am
persuaded that in a review of the strictly scholarly
achievements of Protestant theology in the nineteenth
century, the names of Baur and Harnack will be in the
foreground. Indeed, the more the genuine scholarly

character of theology will be confined to historical theology insofar as it employs general historical method, the more these two will be regarded as the high points of theology as such. Both have founded a dominating school and both have tightly drawn together history and dogmatics and even transformed them into a vital unity. To be sure, the epigones of the Tübingen School, Pfleiderer, Dorner, Hausrath, Lüdemann, Holsten, Hilgenfeld, and others have failed to recognize this; they certainly saw the contrast of which I shall speak in a moment, but they did not locate it properly.

Harnack himself was probably of the same opinion at first. But on reading his Munich lecture of 1917, "On the Certainty and the Limitations of Historical Knowledge," the essays on the period of the Roman emperors and on the relation between church history and universal history, and his later utterances on the general history of religions in his volumes *Out of Scholarship and Life*, one senses a strong approximation to the idea of a general development of the mind (even to Hegel's dialectics), in which the development of the Christian institutions and of the Christian spirit is incorporated.

Today the conflicts of the epigones of the Tübingen School with Harnack's early school are forgotten; they have become almost fruitless. We should rather rejoice in the similarity of the two masters and in the continuity of scholarly principles which is evidenced thereby, and this at a moment when the external conditions of German scholarship raise doubts as to whether this entire great tradition can be maintained, and when the violent spirit of the younger generation, tending toward practical action and excitement, inwardly threatens the seriousness and the power of scholarship as such.

Baur and Harnack: they represent the aristocracy of scholarship; they combined strictest observance of method with a choice sensitiveness of spirit and a kindly readiness for communication, and scholarly nobility with a humanitarian concern for all practical affairs of their fellow men. Today the current of events pulls us away from such intellectual nobility and such objective dependability. Whether forever or only until the principle of scholarship will have been reasserted, this depends upon the general cultural development, our coming political and social destiny, and the spiritual recovery of the German people.

What then, more specifically, is the agreement between Baur and Harnack? It consists in the common descent from the great idealistic-historical method of German philosophy and historiography at the beginning of the last century. The fundamental idea of each is entirely different from the method of older church historians who used to describe a supernatural core of doctrines and institutions (which they regarded as exempt from becoming), only with respect to its historical manifestations and the ways by which it became tarnished or was maintained. Or, in the manner of Gibbon, they interpreted a sequence of illusions and contrivances in terms of common human motivations. This

method is different also from the procedure prevailing
in the school of Schleiermacher and from that Ne-
ander, not to be sure insofar as they described the individual manifestations of a religious feeling-content with
an inward empathy and therefore with justice to all
concerned and edifyingly, but insofar as they pursued
the inner conclusiveness of the all-comprehensive and
all-penetrating development of the power of the spirit.
Also the difference of this method from the procedure of
a literary artist like Karl Hase is quite noticeable: the
difference from the latter's motivational pragmatism and
from his individualizing amplifications in delineating
periods, institutional concretions, and inner processes of
growth. In difference from Hase's artistic brilliance, his
edifying psychologizing, and his dogmatic separation of
profane from Christian elements, the method of Baur
and Harnack is characterized by a constructive synthesis which sees thousands of details as constituting one
great course of development. For this reason, Harnack
never shared Ritschl's judgment of biblical research,
even though he esteemed him very highly, but instead
he joined Wellhausen with respect to the Old Testament and developed the philosophical-historical method
with respect to the New Testament. He agreed with
Ritschl's historiography only insofar as it was derived
from Baur's constructive power as is obviously the case
with Ritschl's periodization of the history of doctrine.
The decisive factor is the affirmation of the general idea

of development, and this is true for Harnack no less than for Baur.

Baur's work is based on the conception of the idea of development in terms of Hegelian dialectics. He presents the history of Christianity as the unfolding of the Christian idea and the Christian idea itself as the climax of the religious-metaphysical idea as such as it unfolds itself in universal history and in the history of the religions. The result is that an autonomous dogmatics is entirely unnecessary, that the whole power and fullness of Christianity becomes visible and effective in its historical development so that the ecclesiastical history of God's incarnation and the explication of Christ, that is, all theology and Christology, become superfluous. The consideration of Christian history replaces all dogmatics because the living truths of the latter lie in the structures of its background and because its vital and effective power is transferred to us and from us to others by historical perception.[1]

Harnack rejected the dialectics and metaphysics which were here assumed and he probably never sensed their magic spell. But he adopted the result. Also for him, theology and church history coincide. Also for him, there are in the last resort no dogmatics and no Christology. He held on to the idea of the incarnation and manifestation of the truth of religion in the entire history of Christianity, indeed basically only there. He too

1. *Anschauung.*

replaces all the subtle and abstruse teachings of dogmatics by the grand view of Christian development in
its main manifestations and through the suggestive influence of great and original personalities. For him, the
substance of the spectacle consists in the consolidation
of the Christian spirit in the great confessional churches
and the national traditions to which they belong; in the
condensation of the spirit of great personalities in institutions and the rise of new personalities from the ruins
of institutions. In what here becomes visible, the Christian spirit manifests its vitality and mobility, something
massively general and individual at the same time, a
basic nature to which it firmly adheres and simultaneously a free, unlimited changeability. All this is characteristic of Harnack's religiousness and of his church
history and theology as well. If Schleiermacher in his
Speeches saw the historical nature of religion as its ultimate quickening power, this is true for Harnack as
well; and if Fichte, Schelling, and Hegel found themselves able to delineate mind only in the extension of
phenomena, this is also Harnack's intention and disposition.

To be sure, he nowhere appeals to these philosophers;
for under the general influence of Neo-Kantianism and
Realism, he is instinctively inclined to reject them. But
all the more emphatically he appeals to Goethe. And it
was precisely Goethe who prior to all those thinkers
suggested this method not so much in reference to history as to the world of nature. He wanted to come to

know the idea and ultimate nature of things in the breadth and fullness of the real, and to see the fulfillment and the law of life in the wealth of personalities. Not dogmatic doctrine, but perception and again and again perception—this was Goethe's keynote. This is a perception which insists upon seeing the nature and "essence" of things and beholds this nature in all that moves and lives.

It cannot be doubted that Harnack's especially emphatic reference to Goethe can be traced to this realism and universalism in the contemplation of becoming, to this sensing of the "essence" of things. Harnack chose one of Goethe's sayings as the motto for his *History of Dogma* and he has made the concept of the "essence" that is visible and alive in history the subject of one of his best-known books. Everywhere Goethe's morphology; Goethe's affirmation of the spirit in opposition to the mechanism of the mathematical natural sciences; Goethe's universal and living contemplation of the moral world is the basis of his thinking. He is entirely steeped in this and he has present in his memory even the most unfamiliar Goethe quotations. Because of this Seeberg has spoken ironically of Harnack's "Goethe-Christianity," and Overbeck heaped abuse upon him because of it. But it is not Goethe-Christianity at all—insofar as one can actually speak of some thing of this sort, I shall presently state what needs to be said; but it is the intellectual background of his conception of the nature of the spirit and its development, the background by virtue of which historical perception can take the place of the idea because it is itself an idea which, at the same time, preserves the concreteness and the incomprehensibility of life. What Harnack, the historian, refused to adopt from the philosophers and what Harnack, the theologian, did not want to take over from the Tübingers, his instinct derived directly from the sources in Goethe.

Precisely from this point of view, the parallel with Baur can readily be understood and explained. Here lies the fundamental difference from Ritschl, the last great dogmatician with whose school Harnack is so often identified and from whom, because of these backgrounds, he is in fact entirely different.

The relation to Goethe, as stated in words in the motto from the *Conversation with Eckermann,* expresses at the same time both Harnack's identity with and his difference from Baur.* If one explains the differences in this way as a distinction within common presuppositions, they must be further specified. One can then say the following: Harnack's historical thinking is empirical rather than speculative, psychologically critical rather than dialectically constructive; and his conception of all

---

* Translator's note:
Goethe's remark, which Harnack uses as a motto for his *History of Dogma,* reads as follows: "The Christian religion has nothing to do with philosophy. It is by itself a powerful entity at which fallen and suffering mankind has from time to time raised itself up again; insofar as one concedes that it has exercised this influence, it is superior to all philosophy and does not need to seek its support."

living (not the abstract scientific) spirit, and therefore
also of the Christian spirit, is intuition rather than rational comprehension, life rather than thought, irration-
al will and quickening fullness rather than rational ne-
cessity and logical formula. The construction which he
too must aim at is more strictly oriented to the evidence
and takes more account of psychological contingencies,
crossings, contacts, and contrasts; and of the depen-
dency of the process upon geographical, ethnographic,
national-psychological, and factual circumstances. He
sees the unity of the process not in a conceptual neces-
sity of development but in the visible and concrete de-
termination by a common ground, and he identifies this
ground or "essence" not with a psychic power which in
the last resort is identical with the highest ideals of the-
oretical knowledge. This psychological realism originates entirely from his historical instinct and sense for
reality; from his artistic feeling for the concrete; and
from his skill of philological interpretation which is
open to individual varieties; indeed from the freedom,
mobility, adaptability, and keenness of his mind, which
are the virtues also of the historians who were and are
round about him. In this sense, he has many similarities
with Renan, to whom he is related specifically by his
sense for style and his feeling for nuances. Also the close
affinity with Mommsen is readily comprehensible.

   To the extent in which he was concerned to justify
this basic position (which he himself regarded as antimetaphysical) and to bring out the contrast implied in

this against the Tübingen School, he liked to appeal, insofar as this contrast was not yet sufficiently explained by reference to Goethe, to the antimetaphysical attitude of Ritschl and Herrmann and to the Neo-Kantians who also defended the autonomy of religion over against metaphysics. But this appeal prevented many, and sometimes even himself, from recognizing the actual nature of things. For what those Ritschlians had in mind was not really the autonomy of religion over against metaphysics, as that saying of Goethe expresses it, but that of supernatural Christianity over against the entire non-Christian world. But Harnack never identifies himself with this contrast; he rather asserted the autonomy of religion as such and therefore also that of Christianity. Actually he has before him a picture of universal history and of the history of religion, where everything is known and formed by entirely identical methods and where, in the sphere of religion, Christianity stands out in virtue of sheer fact by greatness, depth, and power of influence. At any rate, in the course of time, he emphasized more and more this picture which was before him; with this in mind, he demanded in a very remarkable and still highly suggestive speech that universal history should be taught as a course in general education.

What he aims at, as in the case of Baur, is a view of universal-historical development in which Christianity is recognized as a phase of this process of becoming. On account of his psychological-realistic method, the content of this view is different from that of Baur who employed a dialectical-speculative method. In accordance with the affirmation of the decisive significance of the great personalities and their psychologically suggestive influence, he stresses the basic importance of the figure of Jesus rising from later Judaism, and he characterizes the eschatalogical-ethical content of the gospel of Jesus by placing the grace of coming salvation into the foreground and interpreting the grace of the forgiveness of sins by which the hearts of men are prepared for this salvation as a constantly present undertone. The dogma and the foundation of the church, the sacrament and incarnational faith, arise in his view only from Paul's second gospel and from the environmental influences and the psychological characteristics of Paul; he sees in the Christian congregations which resulted from Pauline missions the struggle between eschatological enthusiasm and a Hellenizing process tending to adapt itself to the world, while the Jewish-Palestinian group and its faith in the law are eliminated from the ongoing life of Christianity. Hence the episcopal church with its new canon, its new law, and its Logos-Christology is seen to originate not from the synthesis of Judaism and Hellenism but from the progressive Hellenization in conflict with Gnosticism. State and society gradually open themselves to this new life-organism, and thus there is finally made possible first the alliance and then the integration between the church and the Roman state. In the East, the church remains oriented to the position of the Great Councils, whereas in the West the disintegration

of political power transforms the church into the Papacy, permitting it as a large property owner and as a
great educational power to enter into the history of the
new European peoples. At the same time, the last great
genius of antiquity, Augustine, relatively untouched by
Hellenism, provides the church with a new interpretation of its faith in salvation, marked by many fresh nuances. Also in later times, it is not dialectics, but the
actual course and conflict of forces which determines
the history of the Christian religion, producing especially the separation between Catholicism and Protestantism in which the really determining factors are
again the psychological qualities of Luther.

This is an entirely different picture than that of Baur:
The unlimited active play of historical forces and of
super-rational individualities determines the course of
events, not a conceptually necessary sequence. This is a
theology of historism replacing a theology of dialectics,
lacking, to be sure, the latter's compass but also its ille-
gitimate simplifying conceptuality.

Should one desire to connect this historical thinking
with any philosopher, one can think only of Dilthey,
and, indeed, Harnack mentioned him in his lecture on
"Science and Life" at an important point. Dilthey also
loves to take his orientation from Goethe, and he too
follows the historical idea and method of German Idealism; but after having broken the dialectical structure of
thought he replaces the advantages of logical construc-

tiveness with the benefits of a lively and individualizing
intuition.

In stressing the similarity to Dilthey, I must not fail
to point out the decisive factor which characterizes
Harnack's historiography most distinctly and sets it
apart from every type of historism to which one may relate it. In the case of Dilthey and related thinkers, the
consequence of historism is scepticism, the tragic sense
of life belonging to a highly stimulated mentality which
aimlessly moves about in the wealth of historical data.
But precisely with this, Harnack never had anything to
do. He is a positive thinker who carries about with him
a firm, old legacy of faith. The richness and suggestive
power of history do not deprive him of the sense of direction and least of all of faith in the absolute truth of
Christianity.

For him the nature of Christianity is not that which
all fleeting historical phenomena have generally in common, but the origin, support, and eternal goal of the
Christian development. He radically simplifies this nature by identifying it with faith in God and love for the
neighbor, and he derives its certainty and redemptive
power from the never-failing influence that goes forth
from the simple figure of Jesus. But this nature is for
him the beginning, middle, and end of Christianity, indeed, the perfection of all true humanity. Thus he understands the gospel of Jesus, apart from all merely
temporary environmental factors, as this very humanity

and this is what he regards as that which is decisive in the various forms of Christianity. In his view, it will ultimately unite mankind in a human brotherhood. On this basis, he argues for the need of a reformation, the connection of Christianity with any secular culture which perfects man. Because of this, he was opposed even prior to the First World War to any ethics based upon the principle of the struggle for existence; he was an advocate of peace and Christian community of nations. As president of the Evangelical-Social Congress, he endeavored to reduce and conciliate the class struggle and to establish a platform of common convictions and measures of reform. Against this background, he regarded the person of Jesus as unique. Indeed, this Christian humanity seemed to him so obviously to be the core of all human nature that he had no doubt about its redeeming and liberating power for all nations, also those of the East. Thus he was able to speak of a higher and second nature of man disclosing itself in all this. "As long as the historians of evolution are not yet persuaded of the fact that within the process of development things change, that consciousness and power of will are transformed, indeed, that a new psychological capacity is formed which can function as fully as a primitive power of nature, they will produce confusion and create harm."

He applies the same idea also to Luther's Reformation: "We proceed on the assumption that every man is a moral person and that therefore all that Jesus says is

beyond controversy and signifies a natural attitude. The
objection that at one time it was not possible to speak to
men in this way is not valid: from now on (that is, beginning with Luther) one is able to speak to them in
this way and one must do so. All the authoritative
preaching about God no longer falls upon the wretched
life of men like an otherworldly, foreign power; as the
message about the omnipotent and holy father-god it
rather belongs to the sphere of man's own being. This is
why miracles and ecstasies have had to cease, and the
old religion has had to yield to a new (namely, the Lutheran) one. In it the supernatural has become something constant, indeed something natural."

These remarkable sentences do not signify an apolo-
getical evasion or a false affirmation of the absoluteness
of Christianity, or a means of avoiding the scepticism of
historism. No, they represent the heart of Harnack's historiography and of his religious interpretation of history, and this is for him as natural and indigenous as he
expects it to be for everyone else. In his innermost nature, he is a contemplative and undogmatic historian
who wishes to deliver theology from its hairsplitting
and its laborious tricks, but he is no sceptic and no rela-
tivist. He says somewhere: "The more we recognize that
all things are relative, the more responsible we become."
He performs this responsibility in the sentences we have
quoted, and their melody recurs in everything he has
written. On account of this responsibility, he was so
highly irritated by the relativistic method applied to the

history of religions by Usener and Bousset. For the
same reason, he attempted again and again to overcome
the division of the denominations and to limit the mili-
tarism of the nations.

Most modern men may not find themselves convinced
by this, but for Harnack it constitutes experience and
the self-evident starting point for everything. He rejected Baur's dialectic although it was a weapon against
relativism. Yet he also avoided falling victim to Dilthey's scepticism. The "naturalness" of the gospel understood as a product of development and especially as
an achievement of Protestantism is for him an indubi-
table guide and a self-evident norm. Obviously he thus
goes back behind Hegel and German Idealism to the
noblest ideas of the Enlightenment. Here he is at one
with Herder and Kant and again especially with certain
basic convictions of Goethe who was by no means first
the pagan Titan and then the civilized man full of resig-
nation as modern debunking biographers like to present
him, but whose persistent Protestant convictions and
Christian humanitarianism Harnack has rightly laid
hold of and at the same time enlarged in the light of the
fuller teachings of the Reformation. (Only this is the
true element in the talk about Harnack's "Goethe-Christianity.")

Only if one sees the connection between this affirmation of humanity and the scepticism which is the danger
of historism, can one fully understand and recognize
that Harnack's principles are not derived from reflection

or that they represent the conclusion of a man of letters, but that they are the expression of his thoroughly positive personality.

Thus we can then also observe a contrast to Baur which is no longer identical with that of a psychological realism versus metaphysical dialectics. The idea which, according to Baur, is the guiding and supporting motif of the truth-content of human development is here replaced by an ethical view of humanity reminding one of Kant, Herder, and Goethe but more fully determined by Luther's conception of justification and thereby assuming a specifically Christian character. Harnack too regards this as the goal and outcome of man's development, but in no way as a supernatural creation or as a sheer fact. But the goal is reached by leaps and bounds and in the end by a final leap, and the development is not a purely logical explication of something that has been there from the beginning.

As far as I can see, one cannot object to this modification of the idea of development. In a somewhat different way, Kierkegaard advanced it in his argument against Hegel. It is certainly not proper to speak here of "positivism" or of "unscientific bias." The real reservations one must have concerning this view are completely different ones and they are the following: Is it correct to regard this characteristically European goal of development as the ultimate which all men and nations can adopt for themselves, and is it possible for anyone to orient himself so directly and naively to the figure of

Jesus, regardless of all historical criticism? Anyone who wishes to realize the full weight of these objections must read the *Diary of a Philosopher* written by Harnack's compatriot, the Count von Keyserling, or Albert Schweizer's *Quest of the Historical Jesus.* So far as I am concerned, I should not find it possible to answer the two questions affirmatively. I am unable to accept Harnack's idea of "ethics" and of love insofar as he understands it as an idea that is unambiguous and independent from any metaphysics and is supplemented only by confidence in God as the source of power, courage, and joy. Some time ago, Harnack and I were engaged in a discussion about this which touched our basic presuppositions more deeply than we then realized.

It has here been my purpose to explain the relation between Baur and Harnack as I have come to understand it in the course of time. In order to be complete, I should therefore have to deal also with Harnack's school. But to do this briefly is impossible. Let me only say that this school is plainly divided into two separate groups: on the one hand, there are the students of Patristics who are gathered around the *Texte und Untersuchungen:* they are mostly not interested in the general questions I have dealt with here. On the other hand, there are church historians who preserve and extend Harnack's outline of the history of dogma, men like Loofs, Kattenbusch, Scheel, v. Schubert, Seeberg, and others: they are generally noteworthy because of their advocacy of a more creedal and supernaturalistic position; only in the case of Holl, I believe to observe a certain turning back to Hegel.

To what extent I myself belong to this school, I cannot be sure to say. Nor am I sure how far Harnack on his part would agree that I do belong to it. But what I know is that in that part of my knowledge which is related to church history and the history of doctrine, I am most deeply indebted to him; indeed, I have derived it from his and Ritschl's infinitely productive works. I refrain from describing the great changes which these ideas have then undergone in my own labors. Moreover, I have intended to deal not with my relation to him but with that of Baur, especially in view of the fact that I have come to recognize that I have been influenced by both and thus have good reasons to see the problems with which this essay deals. However, I believe that quite apart from these personal concerns, the problem itself deserves to be dealt with.

All I wish to say here about my relation to the one who is being celebrated is, in addition to what I have just indicated, a word of deep and genuine gratitude for the immeasurable stimulation, and especially for the never failing lively interest which despite all differences Harnack has bestowed upon my musings and questionings. I have always found the humanity which he teaches proven by his actions, disposition, and his readiness for communication with others.

II

Ernst Troeltsch

A Funeral Address delivered on 3 February 1923

by Adolph von Harnack

Eternity, thou word of thunder,
Sword, that pierces the soul,
Beginning without end;
Eternity, time without time,
I am filled with such great sadness
I do not know where to turn.[1]

The prophet Isaiah writes: "The voice said, Cry. And he said, What shall I cry? All flesh is grass, and all the goodliness thereof is as the flower of the field: the grass withereth, the flower fadeth; because the spirit of the Lord bloweth upon it; surely the people is grass. The grass withereth, the flower fadeth, but the word of our God shall stand for ever. Amen."

My aggrieved friends!

In the space of less than two years, our university has

1. O Ewigkeit, du Donnerwort,
   O Schwert, das durch die Seele bohrt,
   O Anfang ohne Ende.
   O Ewigkeit, Zeit ohne Zeit,
   Ich weiss vor grosser Traurigkeit
   Nicht, wo ich mich hinwende.

lost twenty-four full professors and our Academy of Sciences fifteen members, a full quarter of its entire membership. Never before has death entered our ranks so frightfully—and we are perturbed, impoverished, orphaned. Now we are gathered once more around the coffin of a dear colleague, a leader in the realm of scholarship and we must renew the plaint: "The flower fadeth because the spirit of the Lord bloweth upon it." What we are experiencing, what is happening round about us month after month in the common life as well as in our personal existence, compels even the most vital and optimistic one among us to look from life to death:

> All we see changes;
> Day sinks into dusk;
> Joy has its own horror;
> And everything faces death;
> Suffering sneaks into life
> Secretly like a thief.
> We all must part
> From all we hold dear.[2]

Yet even though we must ever look from life into death, we must also learn to look from death into eter-

2. Es wandelt, was wir schauen,
   Tag sinkt ins Abendrot,
   Die Lust hat eigenes Grauen,
   Und alles hat den Tod.
   Ins Leben schleicht das Leiden
   Sich heimlich wie ein Dieb;
   Wir alle müssen scheiden
   Von allem, was uns lieb.

nity: "The grass withereth, the flower fadeth, but the word of our God shall stand for ever." To be sure, this only consolation which the prophet gives to us seems to be a bitter solace; yet it is a real and strong solace. Let it be such also to us as we face this coffin, for it was indeed the word and the spirit of God for which the deceased strove; he sought to lay hold of the permanent and eternal in the flux of the temporal, relative, and perishing.

Ernst Troeltsch was born as the son of a physician in the region where Swabia borders on Bavaria; in him Bavarian-Franconian robustness of life was linked with Swabian thoughtfulness. He took up the study of theology because he was inwardly attracted to it; and he spent his first semesters in a serious and rewarding fellowship of students at Erlangen. Then he went to Göttingen, and there he found the theological master, Albrecht Ritschl, to whom he owed the establishment of his theological conviction. From him he learned what evangelical faith must be and what the churches represent as historical formations; but he soon outgrew the distinctive limitations of this theologian even though he was a strong, notable character. His first scholarly publication is an indication of this. Its theme dealt with that period of Lutheran Protestantism, the seventeenth century, when it was most narrowly confined to itself; but precisely there he demonstrated the points of contact which linked also this period with that general intellectual development which had commenced with

Stoic philosophy; he placed his topic on the stage of universal history.

How did he do his work? This was so characteristically distinctive that I must try to give a comprehensive description of it. First of all, there was his enormous power of consumption; it is utterly incredible what he read, day after day, of the scholarly products of all times and nations, not as a bookworm and pedant, but always by way of a free, lively, and animated exchange with his authors: he was always receptive in order to produce. Secondly, there was his extraordinary ability to learn from others. After Ritschl, there were Kant, Schleiermacher, Dilthey, Max Weber, and Hegel who exercised the strongest influence upon him. In the sequence of his works, one can notice these influences time after time. And even though one can clearly see that, because of his quick temperament, he did not always faithfully reproduce what he had read, he made amply good for this by his ingenious understanding. It often happened that in the course of his reading, he thought of something better, more important, and more comprehensive. The flux of his ideas flowed like a river through the lifework of the great philosophers and thinkers, ripping off from their shores huge parts and bearing them away in its own rolling waves. Furthermore, from the beginning until the end, he was engaged in his studies not only in the presence of his students and auditors but also before the larger public. This should commonly not be done, but he could do nothing else, and he was able to take the consequences which necessarily had to result from the fact that he could not but disclose the gradual change of those of his views which he had not yet thoroughly thought through. He was allowed to do this because on every stage of his development he offered something new and suggestive thanks to the marvelous power of combination which never failed him. This was his greatest strength, this unusual capacity to put each detail at once into the broadest and richest context and to hold ready for every stone the flint with which to produce sparks. But more than all this—the most important part of his scholarly procedure was the respect and the tenderness with which he handled every subject, every living thing. He despised the violence of the rationalists and the rudeness of the systematicians, and he felt himself separated by a deep chasm from all those who do not rest until they have changed each living subject into an unambiguous, rigid thing, depriving it not only of all glow but also of life itself with all its tensions and contradictions.

Rising quickly in his academic career, Troeltsch taught as a professor of dogmatics in Göttingen, Bonn, and Heidelberg. This significant professorship is the most esoteric one in the theological faculty, and those who hold it frequently have only slight relations with other disciplines; but his colleagues and students in Heidelberg became quickly aware of the fact that the new occupant of this chair treated his field in an en-

tirely different way, and, after a short time, the judgment was firmly established that there were no richer,
more comprehensive, and exciting lectures and seminars
than those of this systematic theologian. Young and old
listeners came bright-eyed from his lectures there in
Heidelberg and here in Berlin to which Troeltsch had
moved in 1915 as a philosopher, not in order to change
his field or even his views, but in order to obtain for
himself the greatest possible sphere of action and in
order to be relieved from the special tasks of the theological faculty.

His manner of lecturing and speaking was unique and
at the same time captivating. He did not aim to formu-
late his ideas sharply and concisely but with repeated
efforts and with an overflowing eloquence which was
amply, even overabundantly at his command, he tossed
an observation or an idea to and fro, assailing it from all
sides and putting it in different contexts until it appeared purified and clear. His mind acted like a powerful centrifugal machine or like a rotating drum which
shook and tossed about the subject until it was cleansed
from all foreign parts and loomed up in its own individuality.

And what did he lecture about and who was he? He
was indisputably *the* German philosopher of history of
our time. Indeed, after Hegel he was the first great
philosopher of history whom Germany has produced.
How could he be this? Because he strove to penetrate
the two largest fields of human thought, ideology and

sociology, and to link them with one another as history into a great unity. Ideology—the world which is given to us as a cosmos of appearances—should be transformed into a cosmos of ideas. He was confident that in this he could and would succeed; his limitless field of work was the idea, and his winged tool was the word. For this very reason he did not dwell for long with the primitives and with folklore, with the unconscious and the mystical, with nature and eros; he knew these realms well but he was of the certain persuasion that in order to mean something in the whole of the higher life and not to hamper it, they must be mastered and interpreted by the all-ruling logos. Yet by this he did not mean that one could or should build an autonomous, lofty construct of ideas but that the ideal should find expression in sociology in the world of concrete life with its different levels, formative processes, and economic elements. The ideal, realized in the world itself, should render this world transparent and make it understandable as an historical cosmos of vital power which is governed by ideas just as it is made up of elements. He was concerned to represent the ideas as real *values*, the reality of which is not inferior to that of the economic elements but rather dominates them. In this sense he wrestled with Marx and with every other thinker to whom only economics mattered or who regarded history as a curtain, thus failing to recognize its productive and quickening life.

Did he complete this project and did he fulfill this

task? Who dares ask such a foolish question? Starting afresh over and over again, he made imperishable contributions to the fulfillment of this task, most recently by his great work on historism the first volume of which he completed a few weeks ago. The words by which he concluded this volume are truly his scholarly last will and testament. They demonstrate both the deep earnestness and the modest dignity of his intellectual attitude. They read as follows: "In order to complete the great task of formulating a new philosophy of history, confident and courageous men are needed, no skeptics or mystics, no rationalistic fanatics and no omniscient historians. A single man cannot complete this work. It is, according to its nature, the work of many, first in the solitude of individual persons then in a broader circle. Only from such circles, a new life will rise and it will derive its common power from different points of origin. The most effective means toward such an end would be a great artistic symbol as the *Divina Commedia* once was and later *Faust*. Yet it is a lucky accident when such symbols are given to an epoch, and generally this happens only at the end of such an epoch. But the task itself which consciously or unconsciously presented itself to every historical epoch is particularly pressing for our moment of life. To conceive of construction and reconstruction means to overcome history by history and thus to furnish a platform for new creativity."

To overcome history by history—how often did he

tell me in our conversations: "One must accept his destiny, love, and transform it into something better. What one's goal is to be and how one is to reach it is implied in this attitude." Petty carping or bickering are out— what is needed is the willingness to take risks and to purge and refine!

And now a word about the man himself! He was a wonderful person and a good fellow in the highest sense of this word. There was in him an original power and a fullness of sun and life. At all times he was upright and honest, frank and free; there was nothing contrived and nothing small about him. But—and this was his most attractive and deepest trait—in this powerful naturalness of his, there breathed a quiet, noble, pure soul. As it was his way as a scholar to meet every living being with an open and tender sensitivity, so the core of his being was a tender feeling and a chaste loving-kindness. But it was hidden—and from his impetuous temperament he cast over this core the cover of a heedless freedom. Because he had nothing to hide, he did not wish to hide anything nor to leave anything unoutspoken, and he wished to present himself as he happened to be. We cannot conceal and we do not need to dissemble the fact that he was not easy to live with. He made it difficult for many to accommodate themselves to him, even for those who knew him for a long time and who shared their life with him. He could inflict hurts by his frankness and wounds by his impetuosity. He did not make it easy for anyone to come close to his innermost being. But who can be surprised that the stream of glowing genuine metal which flowed through him also formed into a slag? And then—there were many indeed who were able, sooner or later, to enjoy the whole man in the totality of his being!

The whole man—he believed in the meaning of life and history and in the meaning of his own life: this is the practical test of faith in God. Moreover, he believed that the majesty and humility which shines forth from the cross of Christ is the example and power of our life; this is the practical test of the Christian faith.

Dear, valued friend, we shall not see you again nor hear your voice again. Oh, how bitter this is and how difficult it is to overcome the feelings of nature! "The flower fadeth, for the spirit of the Lord bloweth upon it." But the God to whom you have gone is not the God of the dead but of the living, and his dead live with him. "The word of our God standeth for ever." May he teach us to feel his hand also in want and death, in sorrow and hunger. May he console the grieving widow and may he let the father's blessing rest upon the orphaned son. And may he strengthen us all so that we may learn to look up and to accustom ourselves to the eternal.

> Each day tells the next
> That life is a pilgrimage
> To vast eternity.
> O wondrous eternity,

Accustom my heart to thee.
My salvation is not of this time or world.[3]

3. Ein Tag, der sagt's dem andern,
   Mein Leben sei ein Wandern
   Zur grossen Ewigkeit.
   O Ewigkeit, du schöne
   Mein Herz an dich gewöhne
   Mein Heil ist nicht in dieser Zeit.

Index